Playground Poets

Let your creativity flow...

ode

limerick haiku

rhyme

ball

Northern Scotland
Edited by Bobby Tobolik

D0313235

 Young**Writers**

First published in Great Britain in 2005 by:
Young Writers
Remus House
Coltsfoot Drive
Peterborough
PE2 9JX
Telephone: 01733 890066
Website: www.youngwriters.co.uk

SB ISBN 1 84602 141 3

Foreword

Young Writers was established in 1991 and has been passionately devoted to the promotion of reading and writing in children and young adults ever since. The quest continues today. Young Writers remains as committed to the fostering of burgeoning poetic and literary talent as ever.

This year's Young Writers competition has proven as vibrant and dynamic as ever and we are delighted to present a showcase of the best poetry from across the UK. Each poem has been carefully selected from a wealth of *Playground Poets* entries before ultimately being published in this, our thirteenth primary school poetry series.

Once again, we have been supremely impressed by the overall high quality of the entries we have received. The imagination, energy and creativity which has gone into each young writer's entry made choosing the best poems a challenging and often difficult but ultimately hugely rewarding task - the general high standard of the work submitted amply vindicating this opportunity to bring their poetry to a larger appreciative audience.

We sincerely hope you are pleased with our final selection and that you will enjoy *Playground Poets Northern Scotland* for many years to come.

Contents

Andrew Forbes (11)   19
Caroline McClean (11)   20
Lori Brady (11)   21
Jory Peters (11)   23
Alistair Davidson (11)   23
Adam Brown (12)   24
Bobbi McMillan (11)   25
Emily Spasic (11)   26
Robert Chambers (11)   26
Connor Gardiner (11)   27
Shaun Kerrigan (11)   27
Lauren McNamara (11)   27

Arngask Primary School, Perth
Robert Milne (11)   28
Cameron Nicol (11)   28
Harry Bayne (10)   28
Catriona Donaldson (11)   29
Benjamin Rennie Watt (10)   29
Hannah McLeish (10)   29
Anna Gourlay (11)   30
Emily MacLeod (10)   30
Liam Swanson (11)   31
Hannah MacLeod (10)   31
Hannah McLaughlin (10)   31
Isla Reid (11)   32
Matt Williams (11)   32
Fearn Cole (11)   33
Catriona Sutherland (11)   33
Stuart Elder (11)   34
Steven Millar (10)   34
Scott Andrew (11)   35
Jordan Cummings (11)   35
George Brown (10)   36
Becky Adam (11)   36

Avoch Primary School, Avoch
David Fair (11)   36
Karoline Beigley (9)   37
Ewan Catto (10)   37
Allis Kerr (9)   38

Dominic Dalseme-Stubbs (10)   38
Callum Munro (11)   39
Liam Mackenzie (9)   39
Rebecca Buchan (11)   40
Joanne Stewart (9)   40
Patrick Roesmann (10)   41
Matthew Williams (9)   41
Jessica Hasson (9)   41
Megan Jack (9)   42
Emma Paterson (9)   42
Sarah Miller (8)   42
Savannah Hope (10)   43
Aidan Hersee (8)   43
Bethany Reid (8)   43
Ruth Hersee (10)   44
Laura Kelman (8)   44
Lauren Urquhart (11)   44
Michaela Reid (11)   45
Eilidh Foster (11)   45
James Rigby (9)   46
Nynke Jansen (11)   46
Beth MacDonald (11)   46
Georgia Gubbins (10)   47
Corrie MacNally (10)   47
Megan Davidson (10)   48
Emma McLoughlin (10)   48
Abigail Sked (9)   49
Calum Bassindale (11)   49
Halla Bell-Higgs (9)   50
Laura MacLeod (9)   50
Katie MacLeod (9)   51

Bervie Primary School, Montrose
Daniel Lovick (10)   51
Kirsty Archibald (10)   52
Mhairi Innes (10)   52
Amy Barbour (10)   52
Cameron Donaldson (10)   53
Alana Knight (10)   53
Joanne Stirling (10)   53
Leigh Wilson (10)   54

John Anderson (10)	54
Charles Warwick (11)	54
Alistair Carr (10)	55
Mitchell Dorward (10)	55
Faye McCallum (10)	56
Ciaran Thomas (10)	56
Jack McGuire (10)	57
Joshua Filson (10)	57
Sarah Kalume (10)	58
Mark Lamont (10)	58
Alexander Jones (10)	59
Rachel Criggie (10)	59

Brora Primary School, Brora

Alasdair Cameron (11)	60
Ruth Mackay (10)	60
Willie Powrie (11)	61
John Smith (11)	61
William Robertson (12)	62
Alasdair MacDonald (11)	62
Jack Trumble (11)	63
Nadine Mackay (10)	63
Mhairi MacLennan (11)	64
Calum Payne (11)	64
Steven Sutherland (11)	65
Demii Clark (11)	65
Keely Gibbard (11)	66
Lauren MacBeath (11)	66
Ashley Ross (11)	67

Callander Primary School, Callander

Tom Coles (11)	67
Alice Underwood (11)	68
John MacDonald (11)	68
Shannon Dyer (11)	69
Callum Fountain (11)	69
Shona Harvey (11)	69
Gemma Peebles (11)	70
Colin Hutton (11)	70
Amy Hunter (11)	71
Georgia Parkes (11)	71

Scott Anderson (11)	72
Ben Pritchard (11)	72
Jennifer Tait (11)	73
Kurt Scott (11)	73
Carol Martin (11)	73
Eilidh Allen (11)	74
William Leckie (11)	74
Jennifer Warnock (11)	75
Alanna MacLeod (11)	75
Charlotte Hill (11)	76
Rebecca Davis (11)	76
Christopher Ryan (11)	77
Calum Foulis (11)	77
Nicola Campbell (11)	77
Fiona Wiedmann (11)	78
Michael Ferrie (11)	78
Alicia Cowe (11)	79

Crathes Primary School, Banchory
Josh Paton (11)	79
Amy Longmore (11)	79

Crown Primary School, Inverness
Christie Paterson (10)	80
Hannah Chalmers (10)	80
Sophie Fraser (10)	81
Laura Jones (10)	81
Garry Maclaren (11)	81
Ross Whyte (9)	82
Paul Flint-Elkins (10)	82
Ryan Christie (9)	82
Rebecca Maclean (10)	83
David Wells (10)	83
Sam Henderson (10)	83
Daniel Baillie (10)	84
Shannon Wade (10)	84
Sally Donald (10)	85
Harry Newmark (11)	85
Louise Corrigall (10)	85
Nicole Petrie (10)	86

Douglas Primary School, Dundee

Allie Smeaton (8)	86
Nicola Forbes (9)	86
Aaron Ferguson (8)	87
Callum Wilson (9)	87
Reagan Kesson (8)	87
Courtney Ferrara (8)	88
Melanie Martin (8)	88
Aaron Quinn (8)	88
Darren Young (8)	89
Jemma Sproull (8)	89
Nathan-Lee Brown (9)	89
Lori Doreen Allan (9)	90
Danielle Crawford (9)	90
Jamie Lowrey (9)	90
Michelle Donnelly (10)	90
Chloe Anderson (9)	91
Sally Robertson (8)	91
Gavin Lee Thomson (9)	91
Sarah Murphy (8)	92

Downfield Primary School, Dundee

Sophie McDonald (11)	92
Ricky Warden (11)	93
Leeann Chen (9)	93
Kayleigh McDermott (11)	94
Ryan Peet (11)	94
Megan Connor (9)	95
Hayley MacFarlane (11)	95
Adam Hindmarch (10)	96
Benn Cooper (10)	96
Terri Skelligan (9)	96
Stephanie McDonald (9)	97
Sam Hill (10)	97
Jordan Carrie (10)	98
Danielle Hunter (10)	98
Ashleigh Nicoll (10)	99
Celena Caswell (9)	99
Anil Findlay (9)	100
Jordan Noon (10)	100
Ross McCormack (11)	100

Drakies Primary School, Inverness

Dunblane Primary School, Dunblane

Heather Wighton (7)   137
Andrew Aschaber (8)   138
Gail Steven (8)   138
Jessica Duncan (7)   139
Maegan Barker (7)   139
Lloyd Rumsby (8)   140
Robyn Elizabeth Horton (10)   140
Ciaran Reilly (7)   141
Karly Rumsby (10)   141
Amy-Claire Gibson (9)   142
Jordan Reilly (10)   142
Duncan Peter (7)   143

Invergowrie Primary School, Dundee

Michaela Netto (11)   143
Chelsea Craigmile (11)   144
Jody MacGregor (11)   144
Dylan Powell (11)   145
Kevin Karan Singh (11)   145
Jonathan Gray (11)   146
Ben Falconer (12)   146
Susannah Cummins (11)   147
Megan Syme (11)   147
Elaine Abbott (12)   148
Jack Rodger (11)   148
Jennifer Glass (11)   149
Iona Currie (12)   149
Barrie Pullar (12)   150
Harriet King (11)   150
Christina Boyle (11)   151
Dee Ross (11)   151
Oliver Bowen (11)   152
Lisa Pullar (12)   153
Laura Jackson (11)   153
Hannah Ferrie (11)   154
Michael Ramsay (11)   154
Thomas David Walkinshaw (11)   155
Dean Strachan (11)   155
Ross Peter Murray (11)   156
Alan Valentine (11)   156

Johnshaven Primary School, Montrose

Gordon Kettings (11)	157
Siobhan Anne Clement (10)	157
Calum Tavendale (10)	157
Stewart Niesh (11)	158
Alice Main (10)	158
Holli Smith (11)	158
Connor Graham (10)	159
Fiona Adams (11)	159
Ross Sangster (10)	159
Corey Taylor (11)	160
Kyle Alan Mackie (11)	160
Lynda McConnach (11)	160
Craig Cessford (10)	161

Killin Primary School, Killin

Billie Graham (11)	161
Sarah Lewis (10)	161
Jinny Dowling (10)	162
Jack Gibson (10)	162
David Macaskill (10)	162
Conor Nisbet (12)	163
Oliver Dowling (11)	163
Megan Rhys (10)	164
Kevin McKenzie (10)	164
Dale Pritchard (10)	165
Jordan Farquharson (10)	165
Jessie Menzies (11)	165
Hazel Wyllie (11)	166
Lianne Kennedy (11)	166
Millie Tigwell (10)	167
Callum Watt (9)	167
Luke Melia (11)	168

Lethnot Primary School, Brechin

Hamish Duff (8)	168
Liam Howe (10)	168
Heather Duff (10)	169
Ross McLean (11)	169
Callum Fletcher (9)	170

Megan Tait (10) 170
Connor Gourlay (10) 171
Ruairidh Martin (9) 171
Rebecca Martin (8) 171

Marybank Primary School, Muir of Ord
Helen Matheson (11) 172
Ryan Macmillan (11) 172
Blabheinn Mackintosh (11) 173
Harley MacKenzie (10) 173
James Macleod (10) 173
Matthew Walling (10) 174
Andrew Bisset (10) 174
Iain Stewart (10) 174

Mount Pleasant Primary School, Thurso
Lauren Lafferty (7) 174
Ellie Mackrell (10) 175
Tammy Rendall (10) 175
Caitlin Souter (10) 176
David Ross (10) 176
Kerri Mackay (9) 177
Dionne Sutherland (9) 177
Robert Kennedy (6) 177
Emily J Taylor (9) 178
Ben Leonard (9) 178
Shannon Hawthorne (8) 178
Shannon Dunbar (9) 179
Lisa-Marie Watt (9) 179
Lucas Halliday (8) 179
Glenn Ferguson (8) 180
Sarah Alexander (9) 180
Gemma Cormack (7) 180
Connor Dunnett (9) 181
Savannah Sutherland (9) 181
Kyra Duffy (7) 181
Daniel Sutherland (9) 182
Joanne Rawson (9) 182
Craig Wares (8) 182
Gary Farquhar (9) 183

Kim Anderson (9)	183
Matthew Wood (8)	183
Jay Stevenson (9)	184
Andrew McGregor (7)	184
Jamie McCracken (7)	184
Vicki Davidson (9)	185
Kayla Ross (9)	185
Brogan McLean (7)	185
Lauren Mackay (9)	186
Sophie Urquhart (9)	186
Brandon MacLeod (7)	186
Callum Ferguson (8)	187
Holly-Ann Maree Cameron (9)	187
Connor Murphy (7)	187
Gemma Mackenzie (9)	188
Ryan Riddell (9)	188
Marti Ross (7)	188
Hannah Smith (7)	189
Lucy Munro (7)	189
Grant Robertson-Carswell (7)	189
Ryan Swanson (10)	190
Amy Munro (10)	190
Kris Malcolm (7)	191
Michael Wares (7)	191
Jamie Mackinnon (7)	191
Danny Gunn (11)	192
Steven Firth (10)	192
Liam Elder (10)	193
Lauren Mackenzie (10)	193
Laura McPhee (10)	194
Shannon Swanson (9)	194
Michaela Cameron (10)	195
Kasey Maclean (11)	195
Rachael Canavan (11)	196
Marc Hooker (10)	196
Eoin McCracken (10)	197

Netherley School, Stonehaven

Conan Gavan (11)	197
Rebecca Smith (9)	198

Kelly Dunn (11)   198
Lynsey Angus (9)   199
Ashleigh Welsh (10)   199
Andrew Junnier (10)   199
Stefan Michael Schmid (11)   200
Sonia Moir (11)   200
Rebecca Booth (9)   201
Ian McNeill (9)   201
Bethany Byrne-McCombie (9)   202
Caitlin McMurtrie (8)   202
Emma Smith (8)   203
Rachel Smart (9)   203
Brodie Willaims (8)   203
Laura Mann (9)   204

Plockton Primary School, Plockton
Catriona Galloway (9)   204

Rosehall Primary School, Lairg
Sarah Ruth Fenn (11)   205
Simon Fenn (9)   205
Sophie Marie Baillie (10)   206
Hannah Ekema (8)   206
Hannah Louise Stevens (10)   207
Liah Beth Stevens (8)   207
Liam Spence (9)   208
Jordan Morrison (11)   208

Stracathro Primary School, Brechin
Juman Hamza (11)   208
Innes Cuthill (10)   209
Katie Blewitt (10)   209
Rosie Wilkinson (10)   210
Katie August (10)   210
Emma Ewen (11)   211
Ashley Spark (10)   211
Imogen Sherrit (10)   212
Shaney Allan (12)   212
Cameron Leask (10)   213

The Poems

Kitten Paw

First a tail,
Then two green, staring eyes,
A sandpaper tongue
And a kitty-cat jaw.
But,
Most of all
I like the paw.
I am filled with joy
When I feel the tongue
On my left cheek,
A nibble
On the end of my toe
With the jaws.
Now I come to the end
Of the long day
And a kitten kiss
For me.
I go to bed
And then there's no more.

Siobhan Keegan (8)
Alvie Primary School, Kingussie

The Story Of William Wallace

Scots and English
Waiting to charge
Then *chaaaarge!*
And battle commences
Screams of pain
River runs red with blood
Bodies floating downstream
Dead as dodos.

Rhys Cornfield (7)
Alvie Primary School, Kingussie

Hobbies

Hobbies are not people's things,
Hobbies are people's favourite things.
They make people proud and happy.
My hobby is motorbikes.
They are like a car with two wheels
And no roof.
They zoom round the bend,
Making a really loud noise
That goes *neeeaawm* and zooms off
Through the bendy, not trendy road.
And that is what hobbies are.

Ashley Newman (8)
Alvie Primary School, Kingussie

A Bear

A bear
A bear
Is following
That's why
I flee
I flee
Thump and vaults
The bear comes
He appears
To be
Very, very
Angry!

Peigi Sinclair (8)
Alvie Primary School, Kingussie

The Squished Ladybird

One fine day I had nothing to do,
But this idea just came from the blue.
I went to the forest, where nobody goes,
But why don't they? Nobody knows.

It all went well until I accidentally
Stood on a bug, acting so innocently.
When I realised, it was a bad surprise,
I could feel a tiny tear coming to my eyes.

I knelt on one knee
And said sorry
For not paying attention,
Something I will never again mention.

Poor little ladybird
Only lasted a while,
Now I can't look at a ladybird
While having a smile.

Charley Newman (10)
Alvie Primary School, Kingussie

Baby Dolphin

Baby dolphin screeching
In the breeze.
Poor little dolphin
Lost its mother too.
Baby dolphin, don't you cry.
Searching through the waves.
Suddenly a sweet sound
Scurries through the waves
And little dolphin swims away.

Karys Crook (10)
Alvie Primary School, Kingussie

The Dolphin's Song

In the depths of the ocean
With the sun off the sea,
When dawn is breaking
There comes a melody.

It's the dolphin's song
With a sense of peace and happiness,
It's the dolphin's song
In the sea.

The happiness is bubbling
As she swims along,
With the soothing song
Going on and on.

It's the dolphin's song
With a sense of peace and happiness,
It's the dolphin's song
In the sea.

Jordan Orr (10)
Alvie Primary School, Kingussie

The Black And White Bear

The sound of the jungle
Where the animals live
One big panda sits in a tree
Eating bamboo
With a big patch on his eye
Poor little panda
He can't see a thing
He just wants to cry.

Annie-Jane Sinclair (10)
Alvie Primary School, Kingussie

A Day I Won't Forget

It's summer days
And the sun's up high.
There's a soft patter
And a song
From a distant place.
There's a magical world
I don't know where.
A distant place.
I pack my bag
And phone my friend.
We walk beside the river
Talking softly as we go.
I spot a glimmer
So does my friend.
We walk over.
We walk over together.
Everything seems normal
As normal as can be.
I take one more step
And *whoosh!*
A swirl, a swish
A turn
A thud
Sends me flying
Softly to the ground.
My heart beats so hard
That I can't breathe.
The place, it was wonderful
The sun shining bright.
I will never forget that day
That day I slipped into a new world.

Jessica Convery (9)
Alvie Primary School, Kingussie

The Last Life

I am feeling sick, my blood
Is redder than a rose.

The gates are open, I cannot see
How my friends got me into such a thing.

My love, my world
But the guns are more deadly than my friends
Souls and hearts are
Stronger than guns.

The German race is on
Our mission is to kill
The plane is open,
The field is free,
The gloves are off
And my love is gone.

Antonio Vastano (10)
Alvie Primary School, Kingussie

Football Madness

Johnny passed to Bobby,
Bobby passed to Bill,
Bill passed to Craig,
Craig was standing still.

Craig passed to Mark,
Mark was singing away,
Dave passed to Robert,
They would be playing all day.

Robert kicked the ball at the referee,
See!
I told you this would be
A game of football madness.

Sam Cairns (9)
Alvie Primary School, Kingussie

What We Wear Clothes For

I've got my hat for wearing in the winter,
I've got my jeans for goin' out to play,
I've got my jumper for when it gets cold,
I've got my tie for wearing at school.
I've got my socks for keeping my feet warm,
I've got my cardigan for making me cosy,
I've got my swimming costume for wearing at the swimming pool,
I've got my sandals for wearing at the beach.
I've got my dress for wearing to a party,
I've got my tights for wearing under my skirt,
I've got my dressing gown for keeping me warm before I go to bed,
I've got my nightdress for wearing in bed.
I've got my scarf for keeping my neck warm,
I've got my gloves for wearing when it's cold,
I've got my shirt for making me look smart,
I've got my trainers for running in the grass.
I've got my fleece for putting over my top,
I wear all my clothes all year round.

Eve McCrossan (7)
Alyth Primary School, Blairgowrie

Clothing

I've got my spacesuit for going into space
I've got my firefighter suit for putting out fires
I've got my scarf for keeping me warm in winter
I've got my flippers for going underwater
I've got my tracksuit for going on vacation
I've got my tie for going to school
I've got my trunks for going swimming
I've got my shoes for sprinting round the garden
I've got my boots for going out for a walk
I've got my pyjamas for going to bed
I've got my sandals for walking on the sand
I've got my clothes which I wear for different reasons!

Sebastian Currie (8)
Alyth Primary School, Blairgowrie

What I Wear

I've got my tie for wearing to school
I've got my jacket for wearing outside
I've got my dressing gown for wearing to bed
I've got my slippers for walking round the house
I've got my scarf for wearing on a cold day
I've got my T-shirt for wearing at the gym
I've got my shorts for wearing with my T-shirt
I've got my skirt for wearing at a party
I've got my sandals for walking on the beach
I've got my cap for wearing in the sun
I've got my trainers for running in the playground
I've got my swimsuit for swimming in the sea
I've got my pyjamas for wearing to bed
I've got my boots for walking in the snow
I've got my tracksuit for wearing at cross country
I've got my socks for keeping my toes warm
I've got my leotard for wearing at dancing
I've got my blazer for wearing at high school
I've got my jeans for wearing outside
I've got my shoes for running round the garden
I wear all these clothes in summer, autumn, spring or winter.

Kimberley Stewart (8)
Alyth Primary School, Blairgowrie

My Clothes Poem

I've got my tights for wearing under jeans
I've got my skirt for wearing in the summer
I've got my blouse for keeping me cool
I've got my tracksuit for going out jogging
I've got my jodhpurs for going out riding
I've got my tie for keeping me smart
I've got my shorts for wearing with my T-shirt
I've got my cap for wearing at the beach
I've got my clothes to wear in all seasons.

Eryn Sinclair (8)
Alyth Primary School, Blairgowrie

My Clothing

I've got my sandals for walking on the sand
I've got my tie for going to the school
I've got my pyjamas for going to my bed
I've got my cap for wearing when it's sunny
I've got my slippers for wearing in my house
I've got my swimming trunks for going in the sea
I've got my trainers for playing on the grass
I've got my socks for keeping my feet warm
I've got my scarf for keeping my neck warm
I've got my blazer for wearing to high school
I've got my gloves for wearing on my hands
I've got my hat for wearing on my head
I've got my coat for wearing when it rains
All year I am wearing these clothes, until they are worn out.

Steven Bell (8)
Alyth Primary School, Blairgowrie

Clothes

I've got my shorts for wearing in the sun
I've got my T-shirt for playing in the gym
I've got my coat for wearing in the rain
I've got my cap for keeping the sun away
I've got my swimming trunks for wearing in the pool
I've got my tie for looking good at school
I've got my shoes for wearing on stones
I've got my blazer for wearing at high school
I've got my pyjamas for going to bed
I've got my scarf for keeping my head warm
I've got all these clothes for the year.

Ryan Oliver (8)
Alyth Primary School, Blairgowrie

My Clothing

I've got my shorts for wearing in the summer sun
I've got my T-shirt for when it's hot
I've got my swimming trunks to swim in the sea
I've got my sandals for walking on the sand
I've got my socks for keeping my feet warm
I've got my tie for looking smart at school
I've got my cap for sunny days outside
I've got my coat for rainy days
I've got my gloves to keep my hands warm
I've got my blazer for when I am in high school
I've got my scarf to keep me warm in the snow
I've got my boots for playing outside
I've got my pyjamas for sleeping in bed
I wear these to keep me warm.

Cameron Ramsay (7)
Alyth Primary School, Blairgowrie

What I Wear

I've got my tie on for going to school
I've got my shoes on for playing outside
I've got my trunks on for swimming in the sea
I've got my socks on for keeping my feet warm
I've got my pyjamas for going to bed
I've got my T-shirt to wear with my shorts
I've got my belt for keeping my trousers up
I've got my shirt on for keeping me smart
I've got my trainers on for running round and round
I've got my boots for hiking up a hill
I've got my clothes for wearing all the time.

Connor MacDonald (8)
Alyth Primary School, Blairgowrie

I've Got My . . .

I've got my sandals for wearing on the beach
I've got my tie for wearing at school
I've got my coat for wearing when it's rainy
I've got my cap for wearing at the beach
I've got my flippers for wearing at the swimming pool
I've got my pyjamas for wearing in my bed
I've got my boots for wearing when it's cold
I've got my shorts for wearing when it's sunny
I've got my T-shirt for wearing with my shorts
I've got my cap for wearing when it's hot
I've got my scarf for keeping my neck warm
I've got my socks for wearing when it's cold
I wear these every day, every day, every day . . .

Lewis Comrie (8)
Alyth Primary School, Blairgowrie

My Clothing

I've got my hat for shading me in the sun
I've got my socks for keeping my feet warm
I've got my shorts for running in the sun
I've got my pyjamas for wearing to bed
I've got my tie for wearing to school
I've got my wellies for splashing in the puddles
I've got my flippers for swimming in the sea
I've got my shoes for covering my socks
I've got my scarf for keeping me warm
I've got my pants for putting on my bum
I've got my slippers for wearing in the morning
I've got my belt for keeping my trousers tight
I wear these all through January, February, March, April, May,
June, July, August, September, October, November, December.

Duncan Pogson (8)
Alyth Primary School, Blairgowrie

Cosy Clothes

I've got my shorts to play at the park
I've got my T-shirt to wear with my shorts
I've got my dressing gown to keep me warm
I've got my slippers to keep my toes cosy
I've got my cap to wear at the park
I've got my knickers to keep my bum warm
I've got my leotard to wear at dancing
I've got my vest to wear under my shirt
I've got my scarf to keep me warm in winter
I've got my wellies to splash in puddles
I've got my trainers to go to football
I've got my gloves to keep my fingers cosy
I've got my tie to wear at school
I've got my skirt to wear with my tights
I've got my blazer to wear at high school
I've got my swimsuit to bathe at the beach
I've got my socks to keep my feet cosy
I wear lots of different types of clothing.

Holly Shaw (8)
Alyth Primary School, Blairgowrie

I've Got My Clothes

I've got my swimsuit for going swimming
I've got my pyjamas for going to bed
I've got my skirt for wearing in summer
I've got my tie for wearing in school
I've got my coat to keep me warm in winter
I've got my hat for in the sun
I've got my shorts for going to the beach
I've got my socks to put on my feet
I've got my tights for wearing under my skirt
I've got my knickers for wearing on my bottom.
I wear all these clothes.

Elizabeth Stewart (8)
Alyth Primary School, Blairgowrie

I Wear

I've got my jacket for wearing when it's wet
I've got my slippers for wearing to my bed
I've got my tie for wearing to look smart
I've got my nightdress for wearing in bed
I've got my gloves for keeping my hands warm
I've got my scarf for wearing with my gloves
I've got my hat for wearing when it's hot
I've got my jumper for wearing when it's not
I've got my socks for keeping my feet cosy
I've got my other hat for wearing on my head
I've got my tracksuit for going out to play
I've got my wellies for sploshing in the puddles
I've got my trainers for wearing to a party
I've got my shirt for wearing with my tie
I've got my clothes for wearing all year round.

Rebecca Campbell (8)
Alyth Primary School, Blairgowrie

I've Got My . . .

I've got my T-shirt for playing in the sun
I've got my swimming trunks for splashing in the sea
I've got my pyjamas for sleeping in my bed
I've got my socks for putting on my feet
I've got my sandals for walking on the beach
I've got my pants for on my bottom
I've got my coat for in the cold
I've got my jeans for going over my pants
I've got my tie for wearing to school
I've got my shoes for putting on my feet
I've got my cap for wearing on my head
I've got my clothes for wearing on my body.

Christie Fraser (8)
Alyth Primary School, Blairgowrie

I've Got My . . .

I've got my jodhpurs for riding on my horse
I've got my tie for wearing at school
I've got my coat for keeping myself warm
I've got my gloves for keeping my hands warm
I've got my pyjamas for going to bed
I've got my knickers for keeping my bum cosy
I've got my T-shirt for wearing in the summer
I've got my tie for wearing to look smart
I've got my trainers for going in the garden
I've got my jumper for wearing when it's cold
I've got my dress for going to a party
I've got my wellies for splashing in the puddles
I've got my hat for wearing on my head
But I've got all my clothes for all year round.

Megan Young (8)
Alyth Primary School, Blairgowrie

What Have I Got To Wear?

I've got my tie for wearing at school
I've got my sandals for playing on the sand
I've got my cap for wearing when it's sunny
I've got my shorts for wearing at football
I've got my flippers for using at the pool
I've got my belt for keeping my trousers up
I've got my wellies for splashing in the puddles
I've got my pyjamas for wearing at night
I've got my blazer for wearing at high school
I've got my boots for climbing up a mountain
I've got my hat for wearing when it's cold
I've got my clothes for wearing all year.

Matthew McLauchlan (8)
Alyth Primary School, Blairgowrie

I've Got My Clothes

I've got my slippers for going to bed
I've got my tie for wearing to school
I've got my sandals for walking on the beach
I've got my knickers for keeping my bum warm
I've got my jumper for keeping me warm
I've got my skirt for making me look posh
I've got my dress for making me look nice
I've got my swimsuit for swimming in the sea
I've got my tights for wearing with my skirt
I've got my nightdress for wearing to bed
I've got my blouse for wearing when it's hot
I've got my scarf for wearing in the snow
I've got my dressing gown for coming out of the bath
I've got my coat for wearing outside
I wear all my clothes every day.

Tamara Hamilton (8)
Alyth Primary School, Blairgowrie

Clothes

I've got my shorts for wearing at the beach
I've got my shoes for wearing on my feet
I've got my pyjamas for wearing in my bed
I've got my shirt for wearing at school
I've got my T-shirt for wearing at the gym
I've got my pants for wearing on my bottom
I've got my cap for wearing at the park
I've got my socks for wearing on my feet
I've got my blazer for wearing in high school
I've got my tracksuit for wearing at football
I've got my swimming trunks for wearing in the sea
I've got my clothes for wearing all year.

Ian Fotheringham (8)
Alyth Primary School, Blairgowrie

My Special Clothes

I've got my boots for keeping my feet warm
I've got my tie that goes around my neck
I've got my vest that I take off at night
I've got my cap that I wear when it's hot
I've got my tracksuit that I wear on holiday
I've got my trainers that I use to play football
I've got my swimming trunks that I wear to go swimming
I've got my shorts for on a hot summer's day
I've got my slippers for keeping my feet warm
I've got my jumper for wearing in winter
I've got my blazer for wearing in high school
I've got my belt for keeping up my trousers
I've got my socks for keeping my feet warm inside
I've got my sandals for at the seaside
I've got my jeans for out on the grass
I've got my dressing gown to keep me nice and warm
I've got all my stuff to wear and wear and wear.

Euan Wilson (8)
Alyth Primary School, Blairgowrie

Clothes

I've got my shorts for playing in the sand
I've got my hat to keep my head warm
I've got my T-shirt for wearing with my shorts
I've got my blouse to wear when it is hot
I've got my vest to wear under my T-shirt
I've got my wellies to splash in puddles
I've got my dressing gown to wear in bed
I've got my nightdress to wear under my dressing gown
I've got my cap to wear when it is warm
I've got my jumper to wear when it is cool
I wear all these clothes in the months of the year.

Kirsty Chalmers (8)
Alyth Primary School, Blairgowrie

School Memories

I remember, I remember
Miss Dempster in class one
The paintings we did
I had so much fun.

I remember, I remember
My two teachers in class two
I tied my own tie
I even tied my own shoe.

I remember, I remember
Mrs Smith in class three
The way she wore gloves to use chalk
How I got home and felt free.

I remember, I remember
Miss Ellsworth in class four
The awful times table clock
And she closed the class door.

I remember, I remember
Miss Martin in class vive
The stories we wrote
The way they felt so alive.

I remember, I remember
Mrs Morrison in class six
The French she taught us
And the poems she helped to fix.

I remember, I remember
Mrs Morrison in class seven
We went to Winmarleigh
I thought it was Heaven.

Rachel Williamson (11)
Ancrum Road Primary School, Dundee

School Memories

I remember, I remember
Mrs Dempster in Primary one
My first year of school
Was so much fun.

I remember, I remember
Mrs Hughes and Mrs Tyree in class two
The new things I learned
I didn't have a clue!

I remember, I remember
Mrs Smith in class two
When she taught us the alphabet
The work was so easy.

I remember, I remember
Mrs Ellsworth in class four
My first personal research
It really was a bore.

I remember, I remember
Miss Martin in class five
We wrote a story
And I was surprised.

I remember, I remember
Mrs Morrison in class six
We went to the RSNO
With music, they showed us new tricks.

I remember, I remember
Winmarleigh Hall in class seven
Lots of fun activities
It felt like Heaven.

Jonathan White (11)
Ancrum Road Primary School, Dundee

School Memories

I remember, I remember
Starting in class one
I cried every day
And I needed my mum.

I remember, I remember
Moving up to class two
Lots of things I forgot
Too many things to do.

I remember, I remember
Mrs Wright in class three
The way she used to keep me right
Boy, she adored me.

I remember, I remember
Mrs Ellsworth in class four
When she used to tell us stories
We wanted them to go on for evermore.

I remember, I remember
Miss Martin in class five
It was open day for parents
My gran came and got a big surprise.

I remember, I remember
Mrs Mo in class six
The French she taught us
Got me in a fix.

I remember, I remember
Winmarleigh in class seven
When I climbed Jacob's ladder
I felt like I'd reached Heaven.

Andrew Forbes (11)
Ancrum Road Primary School, Dundee

The Magic Box

(Based on 'Magic Box' by Kit Wright)

I will put into that box . . .
Loads of wonderful wishes and
All the different seasons you can think of.
Also lovely vanilla ice cream cones
Hidden at the bottom.

I will put into that box . . .
A brave knight to fight all the nasty things,
A lovely warm silk scarf
And the warmest fireplace ever to keep the box cosy
So it is always mixed with warm and cold.

I will put into that box . . .
A puppy to keep me company and
A spark of gold,
Also a magic wand so you can
Have whatever you want.

I will put into that box . . .
A bit of the Atlantic ocean
And drawers full of sweeties and
Green, sparkly grass.

My box is fashioned from gold and strong metal
With silver, flaming stripes all over
And it travels all night and all day.

I shall surf my box all over the world
And land my box at home
Where I will keep it safe.

Caroline McClean (11)
Ancrum Road Primary School, Dundee

School Memories

I remember, I remember
Miss Dempster in class one
Making a bunny
Was so much fun.

I remember, I remember
Mrs Tyree in class two
She was really strict
And very funny too.

I remember, I remember
Miss Smith in class three
The way she used to say 'good morning'
At the door to greet me.

I remember, I remember
The wedding in class four
We threw confetti
And shouted for more.

I remember, I remember
Miss Martin in class five
We wrote about pirates
My story came alive.

I remember, I remember
Mrs Mo in class six
With her wild ideas
Her hair needed to be fixed.

I remember, I remember
Winmarleigh Hall in class seven
Loads of activities
Oh, it really was Heaven.

Lori Brady (11)
Ancrum Road Primary School, Dundee

A Child At Christmas

Christmas comes
Once a year.
Sometimes our memories
Forget Christmas past.
This Christmas
Won't be forgotten.

We were enjoying
Christmas dinner . . .

A tsunami was
Plotting . . .

Pulling crackers,
Laughing at the
Corny jokes . . .

A tsunami was
Brewing . . .

We stayed up,
Eating chocolate,
Playing with
Our presents . . .

A tsunami was
Terrorising Asia,
Flooding villages,
Destroying houses,
Killing thousands
Of people.

Families were
Searching rubble
For missing relatives.
The smell of rotten fish
From overturned boats,
Wafted through the air.
Towns needed food
And water.

Dead fishermen
Floated in the water.

People tried to cope
But in their hearts
They couldn't.

Jory Peters (11)
Ancrum Road Primary School, Dundee

Dad

(Father's Day 2004)

I love the way my dad tucks me in bed
And cuddles me till I fall asleep
Sometimes he falls asleep with me
And says goodnight.

I love the way my dad takes me to see the cars
Subarus, Fords and lots of different kinds
He takes me to new places
And sometimes buys me an ice cream.

I love the way my dad loves and cares for me
And makes up funny jokes
He always makes me laugh
No matter what.

I love the way my dad plays with me
And we play football, tennis and
All kinds of stuff and I am lucky
To have the best dad in the world.

Alistair Davidson (11)
Ancrum Road Primary School, Dundee

But Think Of?

Nice warm beds,
With our loving family around us.
But think of the war.
Cold, hard ground as beds
And very lonely people.

Nice warm food cooked in
Nice warm houses,
But think of the war.
Horrible cold food cooked in
The cold, hard rain.

Warm clothes with
Nice warm showers in every house.
But think of the war.
Thin, cold clothes with
Freezing cold showers.

Nice warm central heating
With electricity.
But think of the war.
Freezing cold trenches
With no electricity.

I hear people giggling
And clapping in the distance.
But think of the war.
They hear people dying
And shellfire in the distance.

I see birds in the trees
And busy roads in the town.
But think of the war.
They see death on the horizon
And lots of bodies in no-man's land.

I feel free,
I am free as a bird.
But think of the war.
They feel like death,
They feel like they'll never be free!

Adam Brown (12)
Ancrum Road Primary School, Dundee

The Magic Box

(Based on 'Magic Box' by Kit Wright)

I will put into that box . . .
The bounciest bed ever made
Lots of chocolate only for me
A warm fire to heat me up on a winter's night.

I will put into that box . . .
The most happiness a person could have
A life full of faith and hope
The feeling of safety and security.

I will put into that box . . .
The fluffiest white rabbit
With long, soft ears and little blue eyes
Who feasts on carrots all day long.

I will put into that box . . .
The biggest hot air balloon Man made
With five big splodges of colour
Slowly drifting anywhere.

My box is decorated with gold and steel
With tartans from Scotland and silks from China
Its locks and hinges are Victorian antiques
Polished to look as good as new.

I shall jump in my box
As high as the birds fly
Touching the clouds with my fingertips
Dodging planes and helicopters by inches.

Bobbi McMillan (11)
Ancrum Road Primary School, Dundee

Father

(Hopefully this poem will show you how I feel. Happy Father's Day 2004 from Emily)

I love the way that you make me laugh,
Make me feel like someone special.
You make me feel all warm inside,
I'm glad that you're my father.

I love the way you do things for me,
Buy me games and toys galore.
You make me feel like I'm the only person in the world,
I'm glad that you're my father.

Emily Spasic (11)
Ancrum Road Primary School, Dundee

My Magic Box

(Based on 'Magic Box' by Kit Wright)

In my box I will have happiness for everyone
And faith for everyone too
I will have a gingerbread man, so I never go hungry.

In my box I will have a big dragon that breathes fire
And a warm bed so I can sleep all day and night.
I will have a sun in my box to keep me warm.

I will put into my box a whole series of Friends on DVD
And sharing kindness for everyone.
I will have a beach with gold sand and blue sea.

I will have love in my box forever.

Robert Chambers (11)
Ancrum Road Primary School, Dundee

I Remember

I remember lots in November like Armistice Day.
I remember the way he used to teach me right from wrong.
I remember the way he teased me . . .
He teased me just a little but in a very funny way.
One November he went away . . .
I never saw him again.
So Mum said I had to just remember him.
She said, 'Remember, remember the 11th of November,
a very sad day.
Remember, remember he died in November.'

Connor Gardiner (11)
Ancrum Road Primary School, Dundee

I Remember

I remember when he used to chase me around the house,
I remember we used to watch TV together,
I remember how he giggled with me,
I remember we used to bounce up and down on the beds,
I remember he took me to play football,
I remember he was the best granddad in the world,
Now he's gone, I am lonely without him.

Shaun Kerrigan (11)
Ancrum Road Primary School, Dundee

Dad

D is for dazzling
And the dimple on his chin.
A is for amazing
That comes from within.
D is for my darling dad
Whom I love very much,
Whom I couldn't stay far away from
Unless we kept in touch.

Lauren McNamara (11)
Ancrum Road Primary School, Dundee

Anger

Anger is red, like acid sizzling loudly,
It sounds like the fierce engine of a motorbike,
It tastes like a very hot chilli,
It smells like a fire burning and sparking,
It looks like a bomb ready to explode,
It feels like you're going to pop,
It reminds you of when you lose a race.

Robert Milne (11)
Arngask Primary School, Perth

Fear

Fear is orange, like the burning sun rising.
It sounds like someone whining.
It tastes like weak, watery juice.
It smells like oily paint.
It looks like you're about to get punched.
It feels like running away from someone.
It reminds me of a scary movie.

Cameron Nicol (11)
Arngask Primary School, Perth

Chocolate Marshmallows

Yummy, soft chocolate fall
Tiny marshmallows open and yum
The new, soft taste.

Harry Bayne (10)
Arngask Primary School, Perth

Fear

Fear is white, like your scared, pale face.
It sounds like click-click, your teeth are chattering.
It tastes like a chocolate after your race.
It smells like that cupboard that no one cleans but me.
It looks like that street light quivering on and off, just go look
                                          and see.
It feels like an empty room where everyone should be.
It reminds you of that night - no food, no lights, no TV!

Catriona Donaldson (11)
Arngask Primary School, Perth

School

School is grey, like a great big bear.
It sounds like more work.
It tastes like disgusting, cold cucumber soup.
It smells like dark, stinky junk.
It looks like a cold, wintry morning.
It feels like a hot and sticky volcano.
It reminds me of Primary 5.

Benjamin Rennie Watt (10)
Arngask Primary School, Perth

Fear

Fear is black, like the darkness.
It sounds like you're going to get hurt.
It tastes like cold ice dribbling down your back.
It smells like dark, jammy blood.
It looks like dark mist.
It feels like a shivering person at the North Pole.
It reminds me of scary things.

Hannah McLeish (10)
Arngask Primary School, Perth

War

I can see bright lights flashing everywhere I look,
Men falling all around me,
Machine gun flashes coming from all around,
Blood spurting from the dead and wounded.

I can hear men shouting orders to the soldiers,
Machine gun sounds everywhere,
Screams of people getting shot,
Massive bombs exploding in the distance.

I can feel the long grass whipping against my fingers,
Rain stinging across my face,
My machine gun tapping against my legs,
My heart pounding against my uniform.

Anna Gourlay (11)
Arngask Primary School, Perth

Wartime Blues

Exploding bombs destroying buildings,
Roaring fires across the land
Blood and tatty clothes scattered around
Soldiers running all over.

I can hear exploding bombs
Whooshing round the sky
The banging of machine guns *bang, bang, bang*
Smoke filling the sky.

You feel nervous and think it's never going to end
You're feeling tired, hurt and worn down
You feel upset, angry
A whole load of different things.

Emily MacLeod (10)
Arngask Primary School, Perth

Sadness

Sadness is black, like a never-ending pit of despair
It makes an echo from the smallest sound
And you can taste your salty tears leaking from your eyes
You smell poison sorrow
And your tears make everything look blurry
You feel guilty for your sin
And it reminds you of people worse off than you.

Liam Swanson (11)
Arngask Primary School, Perth

Fear

Fear is grey, like an angry storm
It sounds like someone screaming in tears
It tastes all horrible and foul
It smells like a smoky fire late at night
It looks offensive and extremely vile
It feels like something you cannot face
It reminds me of times when I came home in tears.

Hannah MacLeod (10)
Arngask Primary School, Perth

Happiness

Happiness is pink, like the sky at sunset
It tastes like sweet candyfloss
It sounds like the singing of a bluebird
It smells like bright pink roses
It looks like an empty beach at sunset
It feels like warmth
It reminds me of my family.

Hannah McLaughlin (10)
Arngask Primary School, Perth

The Football Match

I can see the players running up and down the field
Fans with scarves jumping around like idiots
Fluorescently dressed policemen trying to control the fans
And the tomato sauce oozing out of my burger.

I can hear the sounds of the crowd celebrating
The sounds of the opposition's fans yelling and swearing
                                    because we're winning
The sounds of the loudspeakers announcing the score
And the sounds of the crowd singing to boost the players' confidence.

I can feel the hard, blue seat beneath me
My trainers kicking off the concrete steps
The soft, warm feel of my scarf hanging from me
And the sauce from my burger squidged in my hand.

Isla Reid (11)
Arngask Primary School, Perth

Classroom

What can you see?
Bored children fiddling with their pencils
People swinging on their chairs
A child writing in his jotter
People whispering to each other.

What can you hear?
Pencils scraping on paper
The teacher talking
Children talking to each other
The motorway behind me, cars zooming past.

What can you feel?
Putting pressure on my pencil
Interest in what I'm doing
My sore fingers on my hand
And how bored I am right now.

Matt Williams (11)
Arngask Primary School, Perth

Ratty Sewers

What can you see?
Rats scurrying in the dark, deep waters,
Things bobbing in the deep, black, horrible water,
The walls dripping all the time,
Creepy tunnels going off in every direction.

What can you hear?
Rats squeaking in the savage water,
The sound of rushing water,
Small splashes of disease-infested water,
Dirty water flowing through the tunnels.

What can you feel?
Hairy, long-tailed rats scampering over your feet,
The cold seeping into your feet,
The fear of being stuck down here,
The relief of finding the gunge-covered ladder and light!

Fearn Cole (11)
Arngask Primary School, Perth

Forests

Beautiful bronze oaks swaying,
Baby deer chewing nervously and
Jumping the thick, green ferns.

Pleasant black moles digging,
Jumpy rabbits tunnelling inwards and
Escaping the bushy, red fox.

Fat, bright pheasants pecking,
Grey wood pigeons gliding swiftly and
Eating the dry, crumpled seeds.

Catriona Sutherland (11)
Arngask Primary School, Perth

Sewers

I can see
The walls dripping with dirty water
Rats scurrying beneath me
Tunnels going off in every direction
All sorts of things bobbing in the shallow water.

I can hear
The little squeaks of rats
Water flowing through the tunnels
The splashing of the rats' tiny feet
The small splashes of the greenish-black sewage water.

I can feel
The rats running over my cold feet
The confusion of not knowing which way to go
Cold water dripping on my head
The water rushing past my soaking feet.

Stuart Elder (11)
Arngask Primary School, Perth

War Against Terrorism

What can you see?
Fierce car bombs exploding
Citizens of Iraq lying dead
Fierce guns going side by side
Men getting shot at by mini guns

What can you hear?
Machine guns hammering through the air
People shouting at the top of their voices
Bullets booming through the air
People rushing to hide.

What can you feel?
The cold, heavy gun you're carrying
The warm sand you're walking in
Scared of terrorists
The sweat on your head.

Steven Millar (10)
Arngask Primary School, Perth

The War Front

What can you see?
Camouflaged soldiers running for ammunition,
Gigantic tanks firing at their prey,
Shot down men littering the ground,
Huge, red balls of fire soaring in the sky.

What can you hear?
The firing of guns, taking down their rivals,
Dying men shouting desperately for help,
Massive explosions burning my eardrums,
The bossy general shouting out orders.

What can you feel?
The fear of being blown to pieces,
The dry bones and pellets crunching under my boots,
The thick, black smoke blinding my view,
I feel proud fighting for my Queen and country.

Scott Andrew (11)
Arngask Primary School, Perth

War

Planes dropping bombs
Enemies firing at you
Tracer fire flying through the air
Tanks blasting their huge guns

Bombs exploding in the distance
Guns banging
People shouting in fear
Sirens booming

Feel fear of being shot or blown up
The cold rain drizzling down the back of my neck
And the squelchy mud beneath my feet
And the gun rattling in my hands.

Jordan Cummings (11)
Arngask Primary School, Perth

Stables

Stables, stables, what do they smell like?
I think they smell like a hay bale.

Stables, stables, what do they look like?
I think they look like a high, grey shed.

Stables, stables, what do they feel like?
I think they feel like the cold concrete.

Stables, stables, what is that noise?
It's Bertie the horse trotting around.

George Brown (10)
Arngask Primary School, Perth

The Chocolate Pig

Here's a pig that is standing very tall,
He's made out of chocolate, hurrah, hurrah.
The children are hungry,
Staring at the window.
Their cheeks are squashed against the door.
The people are screaming, 'Open the shop!'
And that is it, there isn't any more.

Becky Adam (11)
Arngask Primary School, Perth

Vitamin C

There once was a man from Dundee,
Who took lots of vitamin C,
He became very healthy
And got so wealthy
That now he lives in Capri.

David Fair (11)
Avoch Primary School, Avoch

Sphinx

In the desert there's a sphinx,
It lies there forever and thinks.
The sand on its back is smooth,
But it doesn't want to move.
A sphinx that thinks,
That's smooth but won't move.
It sits next to a pyramid
That has a pharaoh inside,
I don't know why it wants to hide.
He wore a big crown
And always would frown.
A sphinx that thinks,
That's smooth but won't move,
A pharaoh inside that wants to hide,
That wore a crown and would always frown!

Karoline Beigley (9)
Avoch Primary School, Avoch

Get Ready To Fight

I wake up in the morning.
'One, two, three, four,'
I hear marching.
The sun is dawning.
Time to go to war.
Now we have to walk far.
I get my clothes on.
I put on my boots.
I tie them tight.
Time to fight.

Ewan Catto (10)
Avoch Primary School, Avoch

Shopping Time

S aturday morning, it's time to go shopping
'H urry up, Allis!' my sister is shouting
O h no, it's half-past eight, we're going to be late
P lease hurry, we're not going anywhere at this rate!
P leading with joy, my sister is happy
I am sitting in the back with my hair all tuggy
N ine o'clock, we're in Inverness
G etting our shopping, it's a race.

'T his one or that one?' my sister is calling
'I am getting hungry,' my mam is shouting
M e, I am so good, I haven't talked all the way here
E verything is over - that's brilliant to hear!

Allis Kerr (9)
Avoch Primary School, Avoch

Desert

The desert is a dismal place,
Everything is dead, no human race.
There's nothing alive, just bugs and the sun,
Run for your life, sandstorms aren't fun.
Lethal spiders and scorpions alike,
Rattlesnakes just waiting to strike.
You cannot survive the desert's cruel blaze,
Weak without water under the sun's deadly rays.
Farewell, goodbye, it makes the heart churn,
Spiky cactus, lying mirage, may I never return!

Dominic Dalseme-Stubbs (10)
Avoch Primary School, Avoch

Dino Drive

Its rally tyres are spiked iron talons,
Its lights are glowing eyes,
The paintwork as shiny as silvery scales,
The exhaust as ear-splitting as a 'thunder lizard'
(Brontosaurus).
The engine rumbles and shakes the air
Like rattling teeth.
It guzzles gallons of gas
And roars along the track like a raging tyrannosaur.
Hitting a bump, it takes to the air like pterodactyl.
What is it?
A rally car.

Callum Munro (11)
Avoch Primary School, Avoch

Zombies

For zombies life is lonely
But sometimes you can have fun
We'll party till the day has begun.
When dawn has risen we go to bed in our graves
When we are hungry we'll devour a human
When we're thirsty we'll just suck their blood
We'll turn you into zombies too!
We hate those human spookbusters
They try to destroy us.
Life for a zombie is tough
But it's what we do.

Liam Mackenzie (9)
Avoch Primary School, Avoch

Eat More Healthily!

Eat more healthily,
Eat more healthily,
Apples, bananas and grapes.

Eat less of this,
Eat less of this,
Chocolate, sweets and cakes.

Eat more healthily,
Eat more healthily,
Pineapples, oranges and pears.

Eat less of this,
Eat less of this,
Crisps, candy and chocolate éclairs.

This is my poem, now I'm off to play,
But eat more healthily
In every way!

Rebecca Buchan (11)
Avoch Primary School, Avoch

Wild Animals

Lion running mad and free
Monkeys climbing happily
Tigers hunting madly
Forest birds nesting in the trees
Cheetahs running very fast
Foxes hunting in the night
Owls' eyes gleaming bright
Wolves howling at the moon
Elephants squirting water to have a bath
Birds of prey in the mountains
Squish, splat, crunch goes the elephant
Giraffes going *mmmm* when eating green leaves.

Joanne Stewart (9)
Avoch Primary School, Avoch

Titans

They are tall
And they command lots of armies over the universe.
They are known as destroyers
And can only be defeated by other Titans
That have more power than them.
Heroes can destroy weak Titans
But not Gaia or Kronos.
Kronos tried to kill the goodies
But failed and got destroyed by Gaia.

Patrick Roesmann (10)
Avoch Primary School, Avoch

Pets

Purring cat sitting on the couch.
Barking dog sleeping in the lodge.
Swimming fish swimming in the fish bowl.
Hopping rabbits eating lots of carrots.
Talking parrot pecking at the door.
Little puppy lying on the floor.
Small hamster chewing at the door.
Tiny kitten running across the floor.

Matthew Williams (9)
Avoch Primary School, Avoch

Dolphin

Dolphin, dolphin, swim in the sea,
Can you come and play with me?
I love your shiny blue and grey skin
And the way you jump out and in.
I wish I could swim with you
And see if the sea is really blue.

Jessica Hasson (9)
Avoch Primary School, Avoch

My Dog

Running through the fluffy snow
His legs go so fast
I could never do that, I would never last
He dives into the pond
With a great big splash

He gets all wet and cold
And runs into the park
I know that he is my dog
Because he is called Lark.

Megan Jack (9)
Avoch Primary School, Avoch

Pets

Horses like running
Dogs like barking
Cats like miaowing
Birds like tweeting
Rabbits like sniffing
Fish like swimming
Foxes like hunting.

Emma Paterson (9)
Avoch Primary School, Avoch

Dolphins

Dolphins' skin is blue and grey
They like to jump, they like to play.
They swim in the deep blue sea,
Eating fish for their tea.

Sarah Miller (8)
Avoch Primary School, Avoch

5th Of November

Bonfire burning blissfully,
Rushing rockets raging around,
Hoods hopped up against the rain,
Children chewing candyfloss,
Crazy colours curling off Catherine wheels,
Glimmering glowsticks gazing about,
Freezing frost floats down,
Golden rain glittering gracefully,
Roman candles rising upwards,
Flares flying forwards,
A party of parachutes panic into the sky,
Guy Fawkes just burnt out and time to say bye bye.
Goodnight.

Savannah Hope (10)
Avoch Primary School, Avoch

Ships And Boats

Boats, boats, they row, they float,
They take a while to start.
If you were on a boat
You would know how it feels.
I'm telling you, it is scary,
As scary as can be.

Aidan Hersee (8)
Avoch Primary School, Avoch

Dolphins

Dolphin, dolphin, laugh and play,
Dolphin, dolphin, have fun today.
Dolphin, dolphin, swim and swim,
Let's see you jump out and go back in.

Bethany Reid (8)
Avoch Primary School, Avoch

Bonfire Night

Crackling, crazy, creaking Catherine wheels
Whizzing round and round.
Babies bawling loudly.
Bonfire burning briskly.
Children chomping cheeseburgers.
Fireworks flashing fiercely.
Roman candles filling the sky with stars.
Teeth chattering in the November cold.
Rockets rushing right up into the sky.

Ruth Hersee (10)
Avoch Primary School, Avoch

Lighthouse

It's shining bright
And it's timing's right.
A spark in the dark,
Light leaves its mark.
A stripy cylinder
And a beam of light,
Guarding sailors
Through the night.

Laura Kelman (8)
Avoch Primary School, Avoch

Happiness

Happiness is like opening presents on Christmas Day.
It feels like the beginning of the school holidays.
It sounds like the waves splashing on the beach.
It smells like your favourite meal.
It reminds me of hugs from my granny.

Lauren Urquhart (11)
Avoch Primary School, Avoch

Hope You Enjoy The Fireworks!

Catherine wheels circling into the lonely, dark sky
Children crying as the fireworks crackle and crash
Babies wailing while the whistling rockets rush into
The sparkling sky
Sparklers blazing and flickering
Bangers sizzling and booming into the night sky
While the crowd watch with glee
People standing in front of the bonfire
The flames thunder, spark, crackle and crack
To keep them warm
The stars flicker and flash
Fireworks burst and glitter in the darkness
Hope you enjoy the fireworks tonight
With the dark, starry sky.

Michaela Reid (11)
Avoch Primary School, Avoch

Bonfire Night

A roar of rockets screeching into the sky.
Sparklers dazzling in the night,
While the flaming fire burns like a rockets
Fading away in the distance.
Catherine wheels crackling crazily
As they go whizzing round and round.
The Roman candles spurting out countless colours
While the crackers sizzle
As they drift into the sky.

Eilidh Foster (11)
Avoch Primary School, Avoch

Stirling Bridge

As Wallace and de Moray clank on
My heart starts to thunder
I'm sweating like a tap
I have a terrible feeling that I will not be alive!
I'm shaking all over, but I look at my leaders and it calms me
I am terrified that spears will pierce my heart
Like a kebab on a skewer at a party
Arrows might pass through me and take chunks from me
The Scottish army might have a bad time, but there's always hope.

James Rigby (9)
Avoch Primary School, Avoch

Anger

Anger is blue, a burning hot, flaming fire.
It sounds like a huge wave crashing over two kids.
It smells like mould growing on a sweet strawberry.
It feels like a thousand bee stings in your mouth.
It tastes like mushrooms and Brussels sprouts
Being crammed down your throat.
Anger reminds me of darkness
Wrapping its cloak around the fire.

Nynke Jansen (11)
Avoch Primary School, Avoch

Anger

Anger smells like a burning fire,
It sounds like lightning showering the sky,
It tastes like limes and towers of salt,
It feels like the Devil arriving at your shoulder.
It's as green as the knife-like thorns on a rose bush,
It reminds me of the raging eye of a charging bull.

Beth MacDonald (11)
Avoch Primary School, Avoch

The Silent Wait

The waves,
Slowly coming up
To the awaiting pebbly beach,
Covered in seaweed,
Pieces of wood from old shipwrecks.
Fog appears over the boathouse,
Then drifts over the harbour.
The boathouse,
Full of old ships' compasses,
Or maybe the odd shark's tooth.
The fog thickens,
I see no ships.
The gulls left hours ago.
Now, lightly poised, the rising oar
The bow of the boat slits through the waves,
Slowly coming past the creaking pier
And into the silent harbour.
The gulls come back now,
The fog clears,
Everybody rushes to the harbour
And hopes that the sailors have survived
The foggy night at sea.

Georgia Gubbins (10)
Avoch Primary School, Avoch

'No' Is A Red Word

As red and disgusting as a rotting tomato,
As revolting as stinking fish.
It is so powerful, it can stop a life.
It hits you like a brick.
It can cut up hopes like a knife through hot butter.
It is as destructive as a tank
And as hot as boiling fat.

Corrie MacNally (10)
Avoch Primary School, Avoch

The Chocolate Rebel

Eat an apple a day,
They say.
Not true,
They're bad for you!
If you like chocolate,
You know you can't stop it,
You have to . . .
Eat! Eat! Eat!
Munch! Munch! Munch!
Crunch! Crunch! Crunch!
Mmmmmm!
(You get that warm feeling in your tum!
Then have more tomorrow!)

Megan Davidson (10)
Avoch Primary School, Avoch

My Friends

Megan is a chum.
Nicola likes plums.
Rebecca is funny.
Collette likes bunnies.
Danika is silly.
Rebecca likes Millie.
Caitlin is cool.
Hollie has a pool.
Mytchall is weird.
Glenn likes beards.
Luke loves football.
David is small.

Emma McLoughlin (10)
Avoch Primary School, Avoch

The Rainforest

Here I am in the rainforest
With the rain trickling over my body.
There is so much to hear
If you listen hard.
The noises of everyone.

Here I am in the rainforest
With the rain trickling over my body.
There is so much to see
Just have a quick look.
The monkeys, the birds, the frogs.

Here I am in the rainforest
With the rain trickling over my body.
There is so much to taste
Just pick one or two
Of the berries of lovely tastes.

So here I am in the rainforest
The rain trickling over my body.
I like everything here,
This is my home,
For I am a snake.

Abigail Sked (9)
Avoch Primary School, Avoch

Locomotion

A train is a giant caterpillar
Packed with little ants.
A train is a beating heart,
Regularly pumping itself station to station.
A train is a burning cigarette
Continually puffing foul fumes.
A train is a fugitive
Always on the run.

Calum Bassindale (11)
Avoch Primary School, Avoch

Sunny Summer

Here I am sitting in the grass
With the summer sun shining on me
And the buzzards gliding swiftly above me.
There's trees swaying in the breeze
And children playing in the sun.

Here I am sitting in the grass
With the summer sun shining on me.
There is so much around me that I can feel
The summer breeze on my neck
And happiness all around me.

Here I am sitting in the grass
With the summer sun shining on me.
You can hear all around you
The bluebirds singing sweetly
And the children laughing cheerfully.

Halla Bell-Higgs (9)
Avoch Primary School, Avoch

Wild Animals

Apes swing softly on the tree vines
Alligators snap fiercely at their food
Tigers prowl through the long grass
Cheetahs run after their prey
Eagles fly through the air
Elephants stomp away from the crowd
Turtles swim through the calm water
Snakes slither above the desert road
Monkeys eat their bananas
Parrots speak back at you
Snow leopards dive in the snow
Otters glide down the riverbank
Dolphins jump out of the water
Wolves howl at the moon.

Laura MacLeod (9)
Avoch Primary School, Avoch

My Rabbit

Sitting waiting for someone to buy me,
I'm getting sick of lettuce.
Carrot is my favourite at the moment.
Finally, someone buys me and takes me home.

Sitting in my hutch getting kind of tired,
Being praised by my owner.
Watching the world go by,
People staring in at me,
That will never do.

Katie MacLeod (9)
Avoch Primary School, Avoch

Staring Into Space

As I look through my telescope,
It's amazing what I see.
I see asteroids and stars
And Mars, red as red can be!

I decide to go exploring
And I'll set off into space.
I set off in my rocket,
To find a whole new race.

I whiz through all the asteroids
And I whiz through all the stars.
I land my rocket and get out,
I realise I'm on Mars.

I see all these green men,
I say hello and one replies,
'Hi, my name is Glen.'
I take Glen back to Earth and he likes it very much!
So the next day I go to Venus and
The adventure happens again!

Daniel Lovick (10)
Bervie Primary School, Montrose

Love

Love is baby pink.
It tastes like chocolate.
It smells like fresh flowers.
It looks like flowers in the wild.
It sounds like singing.
It feels like happiness.

Kirsty Archibald (10)
Bervie Primary School, Montrose

Pain

Pain is red,
Pain tastes like chilli sauce,
Pain smells like milk that's gone off,
Pain looks like a volcano erupting,
Pain sounds like someone screaming,
Pain feels like getting boiling water poured over your arm.

Mhairi Innes (10)
Bervie Primary School, Montrose

Happiness

Happiness is yellow,
It tastes like chocolate,
It smells like a fresh spring morning,
It looks like an ice cream,
It sounds like a bird singing.
Happiness feels like fur going across your face.

Amy Barbour (10)
Bervie Primary School, Montrose

Embarrassment

Embarrassment is red,
It tastes like hot spices,
It smells like a hot cup of tea.
Embarrassment looks like a fire,
It sounds like people laughing at you.
Embarrassment feels like you're turning into fire.

Cameron Donaldson (10)
Bervie Primary School, Montrose

Love

Love is pink,
It tastes like candyfloss and chocolate.
Love smells like a morning breeze,
It looks like a lovely blossom tree.
Love sounds like a mermaid singing,
It feels like a soft, fluffy rabbit.

Alana Knight (10)
Bervie Primary School, Montrose

Calmness

Calmness is blue,
It tastes like chocolate.
It smells like candles burning,
It looks like the ocean.
It sounds like soothing music,
Calmness feels like when you're dreaming.

Joanne Stirling (10)
Bervie Primary School, Montrose

The Red Planet

It is enormous and red,
It reminds me of the boiling sun,
It looks like tomato ketchup with bread,
It is as hot as a hot cross bun.
It is thought that little green men used to live there,
Nobody knows if it is true or not,
Or if Martians had any hair.
It is as red as a Ford car.
The only planet it can be is Mars.

Leigh Wilson (10)
Bervie Primary School, Montrose

Happiness

Happiness is yellow,
It tastes like a sweet cookie,
It looks like a bright sunrise,
It sounds like beautiful music.

Happiness feels like water
Going through my fingers.

John Anderson (10)
Bervie Primary School, Montrose

Pain

Pain is black,
It tastes like stale bread and Brussels sprouts,
It smells like rotten eggs.
Pain looks like a dagger with blood on it,
Pain sounds like a screaming woman,
Pain feels like a rip down your body.

Charles Warwick (11)
Bervie Primary School, Montrose

A Typical Day

I woke up this morning
And Saturn was right in my face.
I woke up this morning
And I was floating in space.
I drove to mars
In my bright red car,
I saw a little green man
In a tiny green van.
I asked him if he wanted to play cricket,
He said he would get the wicket.
We looked at the sky
And saw the stars shoot by.
I drove home
And parked at the Millennium Dome.

Alistair Carr (10)
Bervie Primary School, Montrose

The Planets

5, 4, 3, 2, 1! We are off into space.
When we are further up, I look to the left -
I see Venus, a yellowish planet.
Then I look to the right -
I see Mars, also called the red planet.

We zoom on at the speed of light.
We suddenly stop -
I look out the window.
There goes Jupiter with 16 moons.

We are travelling through space.
I tell the captain to stop.
I put on my spacesuit
And go outside.
I'm walking on the rings of Saturn.

Mitchell Dorward (10)
Bervie Primary School, Montrose

My Journey To Space

Zooming through the air,
Seeing all the planets,
Mercury, Uranus and Mars.
Look, there's the sun,
The biggest of the stars.
The stars are really bright,
But no way as bright as our sun.

Pluto at the back, the smallest one of all,
If you see it alongside Jupiter, you'll see how small it is.

We're taking up for landing, *boom!*
I think we've landed.
Yes, we're on Mars.
I can see shooting stars above my head.

Time to go home,
I'll never forget my journey into space.

Faye McCallum (10)
Bervie Primary School, Montrose

Space

Space is endless,
In space there are galaxies,
In galaxies there are solar systems,
In solar systems there are planets.
Our planet is Earth.

Space is the last thing for man to conquer.
Space is endless.
Is it quiet? We don't know,
For space is space.

Ciaran Thomas (10)
Bervie Primary School, Montrose

The Space Race

Lying on my bed,
Dreaming about space,
I fall asleep.
I wake up,
Now I'm in a space race.
Zooming and turning,
Going about 10,000,000mph.
Yes, I'm first!
Wait, someone just overtook me
Shouting 'Flower power'.
Oh no! Now I'm last.
I just hit a meteor with a blast,
Then I fell out with a *boom!*
Then I woke up
And I was back in my bedroom.

Jack McGuire (10)
Bervie Primary School, Montrose

Spaceship Go Boom

I'm in a spaceship
About to blast off,
5, 4, 3, 2, 1
Is all I can hear.

I can see Mars and comets hitting the Earth.
I can hear meteorites flying past us
And *aliens* talking.
Noooooooo!
We're about to
Hit a com . . . et!
Not again *boooom!*

Joshua Filson (10)
Bervie Primary School, Montrose

My Spectacular Dream!

As I journey through space,
Look what I see -
I see a galaxy,
All creamy and dark
And milky as can be.

Suddenly I see a star
And it makes me stop to think.
Why do we fight
When we are living in a Milky Way?
All creamy and soft,
At the touch of your mouth.
Open wide, so you don't miss out!
Don't worry about rotting your teeth,
Because they've got Orbit . . .
Wait a second - and lots of it too!
So your breath will stay fresh
And so will you.

The Martians are pleasant,
Call them aliens if you please,
I don't really mind, they're not me.
We ate our moon burgers
And said our goodbyes,
We headed for home
On a space rocket ride!

Sarah Kalume (10)
Bervie Primary School, Montrose

Space

Space is enormous and black.
Space rocks are zooming and booming.
Mysterious planets being lost and found.
The sun is burning, popping and blazing.
Stars all silvery and glowing.
Supernovas exploding.

Mark Lamont (10)
Bervie Primary School, Montrose

A Visit To Space

5, 4, 3, 2, 1, *blast off!*
Up we went, high as can be,
Till we got to the edge of the galaxy.
There what we found
Was an alien land,
There were five great big lads
And my mother's hat.
How did they have it?
I don't know -
Maybe it came from a radio phone.
Next, what we found
Was a passing hound.
Space is so vast
And we were there at last.
So we went back
And took the hat.
That was that,
As exciting as can be.
We enjoyed it -
And my mother will be pleased!

Alexander Jones (10)
Bervie Primary School, Montrose

Flying Through Space

I can see all nine planets now,
I know which one I would like to visit,
I think it is the ringed planet, or is it?

Saturn is the ringed planet,
It's colourful and bright,
Even all through the night.

I can feel the bubbling heat of the sun,
I want to get to Saturn quick, so I try to run,
But I can't.

Rachel Criggie (10)
Bervie Primary School, Montrose

Battle Of World War Two

Running into combat,
People dying, guns firing,
Air raids, explosions, banging!
Hiding in trenches, trying to survive,
Tortured Jews, killed by Germans.
Uniforms covered in blood and mud,
Shivering children and terrified adults.
People singing to cheer up the children,
While others are dying of starvation.
Gloomy clouds overhead,
Worn men come home.
Nervous people wait,
Silence as the war ends.

Alasdair Cameron (11)
Brora Primary School, Brora

War

Run, run!
Run for your lives.
Bombs dropping all around,
Put your gas masks on quick,
People all around me coughing,
Choking!
Suddenly, quiet!
The silence is closing in,
The dust subsides
And reveals
That I am one solitary soldier,
Standing alone
By the seaside.

Ruth Mackay (10)
Brora Primary School, Brora

Air Force

Engines roaring,
Bombs dropping heavily.
People running to the underground.
British Spitfires chasing German Messerschmitts
Over ruined land and bloody seas,
Trying to shoot them out of the sky!

People choking,
Planes being launched from aircraft carriers,
Trying to bomb Berlin.

Marines using anti-air vehicles,
Shooting Messershmitts from the dark, gloomy sky.
Dropping lethal gas bombs,
Spitfires being launched from worn airfields.
Off to fight in the war.

Willie Powrie (11)
Brora Primary School, Brora

The War

Men running,
Machine guns firing,
Dead soldiers lying in the mud,
Giant, roaring planes flying overhead.
Men being bombed and killed,
Frightened children screaming and crying,
Exhausted soldiers in the muddy trenches.
Hungry Jews going into concentration camps
And being gassed.
Soldiers singing war songs,
Sad people going into gloomy tunnels.

John Smith (11)
Brora Primary School, Brora

End Of The War

Dad's coming back,
Everyone is happy.
No more crying or evacuation,
Everyone is dancing.
No more blood or dead bodies,
Just sun shining.
No more bombing,
Homes getting rebuilt.
No more war,
Just kind, happy people.
Kids can go out without worrying.
No more gas masks,
Families happy,
Clean water to drink.
War no more!

William Robertson (12)
Brora Primary School, Brora

Start Of World War Two

At the start,
Terrible, really scary,
Bombs, frightening,
Big and loud,
People terrified of the noisy, big Germans.

People stay in houses,
British people killed,
German people killed,
Death!

Alasdair MacDonald (11)
Brora Primary School, Brora

The Gore Of War

Blood and guts,
Blown up huts,
People getting thrown.

War is like two buttons,
One says slow and painful,
The other, quick and easy.

Air raid,
Quick run!
Oh no!

Bang! Boom! Bang!
This is all you hear,
Enemy bombers are coming near.

Now the war is over,
We all look for the four-leaf clover,
Watching the doves at the white cliffs of Dover.

Jack Trumble (11)
Brora Primary School, Brora

Underground

Worried, nervous,
Scared going to get bombed!
Singing war songs,
Enemy planes going over,
People crying with hunger,
Screaming with fright,
Huddled in muddy, wet, mouldy corners,
Dark, gloomy, can't see a thing!
Hiding in case get bombed,
Can't get to sleep with noise.
Waking up, shivering with coldness,
Making sure all safe.
Never-ending!

Nadine Mackay (10)
Brora Primary School, Brora

Underground

Dark, cold, like a deserted alley.
Wet, muddy, never-ending.
Scared, hearing the air raids.
Wanting their families all the time.
Deep down in big holes, never getting seen.
Messerschmidts flying in the sky, dropping bombs.
Air raid sirens going off, *loud!*
Every day inside! Scared!
No one knows where we are,
The underground was near to us.
I could see no lights,
I was wet and hungry,
It was a never-ending war.
I do not know where anyone is,
I think I am all alone!

Mhairi MacLennan (11)
Brora Primary School, Brora

The Air Raid

It was a rainy day,
Feet were getting stuck in the muddy ground.
Bullets were firing fast!
Flies were flying all over bloody bodies,
People were screaming *help!*
Bombs exploding in our faces,
The guns were very noisy!
Planes were flying over the underground,
The gloomy gas was flying over.
Never forgetting him, coughing horribly,
Coming out of the gas, turning green,
Grassy-green.

Calum Payne (11)
Brora Primary School, Brora

Start Of The War

Bombing, burning houses
Blood, guts!
Pain and upset,
Shattered bodies.
Raining bombs on cities!

Cold and loud deaths!
Spitfires roaring in the air,
People torn apart.

Sirens going for air raids.
Brave soldiers getting shot.
Exhausted, frightened soldiers,
Slow, painful deaths.
Scary noises, bombs whistling to the ground.

People choking on green gas,
Wet, gloomy, dirty water!
Will it ever end?

Steven Sutherland (11)
Brora Primary School, Brora

World War Two

It was deserted, dark and cold,
I was left alone
While everyone else was in the dark, gloomy underground
With no light to see or food to eat.
The air raid sirens were going really fast.
I heard planes coming closer to bomb the place.
I hid under a bundle of grey, slimy boulders.
The planes came lower and bombed us,
But I was safe.
I wanted to move to a comfortable position,
I was terrified.

Demii Clark (11)
Brora Primary School, Brora

Underground

Very dark, scary.
People singing sad songs
Silently.
Gas masks on their hunched backs,
In boxes.
People crying with
Starvation.
People in gloomy corners
Lonely.
Planes noisily bombing
Outside.
People shivering with
Coldness.
Some are hiding in case they
Die.
People miserable without their
Family.
People unhappy, in pain.
Suddenly,
Silence!

Keely Gibbard (11)
Brora Primary School, Brora

War

War is people screaming and running,
Countries coming over to bomb.
Children crying, lost!
Bodies lying in puddles of blood,
Gas floating around.
Engines roaring from planes,
Children getting evacuated.
People coughing terribly,
Exhausted, full of mud.
Frightened!

Lauren MacBeath (11)
Brora Primary School, Brora

War

Muddy, smelly trenches.
Going to the underground every night,
Blackout windows,
So Germans don't know you're there.
Bangs! Blasts! As bombs fall down,
People dying, hearts breaking.
Planes flying over.
Worried mums, nervous children,
Cold, bare feet,
Carrying boxes with gas masks in.
Nearly ended, but not yet.
Dark, smoky skies,
Only some husbands coming home
For the end of *war!*

Ashley Ross (11)
Brora Primary School, Brora

The Tree I Know

The tree I know is straight and sway-like,
Its bark is like silver with lumps and holes all round.
The branches are like a hard broom.

Its roots keep it from falling down,
They look like straight, hard sticks.
The hill which it stands on is near my house.

At Christmas it's covered in snow,
The ground all around like a slippery slope.
Everything around almost frozen.
The sun will melt it soon.

I hope this tree will never die,
Or people cut it down.
I like it all year round.

Tom Coles (11)
Callander Primary School, Callander

The Changing Seasons

Watching the world all year round,
Friend in the day, scary at night.
Struggling to break the chains holding me to the ground,
Gnarled, crooked fingers; long, grabbing toes.
Crimson, yellow and orange descendants floating to the ground.
Summer brings light and warmth,
Visitors coming for walks passed me.
We watch our children crowd the forest,
Destined to live like us.
The sun fades and night comes.
We are covered in a blanket of black
From head to toe.
A roaring sound echoes through us
And the earth rumbles.
Then we wave goodbye
As our fate saws through us.

Alice Underwood (11)
Callander Primary School, Callander

The Tree In The Shadows

The tall, dark tree towers above me,
As black as ebony,
Blocking out the sun.
Watch the beams of light burst through the branches,
The shadows flood the ground.
The only sound is the water,
Slowly flowing down the stream.
This was once my hut,
My cousins, brother, sister and I built it.
The tree used to hold it up,
I felt very secure as I sat in my hut.
I could trust this tree.
When I get to the tree, I just rub the moss in my hands.
I've had an exciting adventure and I am going home.

John MacDonald (11)
Callander Primary School, Callander

The Fearful Tree

I was feeling frightened and fearful,
As I crept by, the tree cracked and creaked.
The leaves were shuffling and crunching as I tiptoed by.
The birds were scrambling
Like the bugs scuttling along the ground.
The twigs tangled tightly as the wind flew by,
Making a dark, shady shadow around me.
The beautiful brown colour you see in the day
Turned into fear at night.

Shannon Dyer (11)
Callander Primary School, Callander

The Tree At The Bottom Of My Garden

There is a tree at the bottom of my garden,
beside the blossoming bush,
In my garden there is a tree that stands big and tall,
The tree in my garden has been there all my life,
The blossom on the bush spreads onto the tree,
The leaves on the tree dance to the ground,
At night the tree doesn't make a sound.

Callum Fountain (11)
Callander Primary School, Callander

There Is A Tree

There is a tree, where I used to play,
That tree should be there forever to stay.
There is a tree with gigantic roots,
Up in the branches a pigeon hoots.
There is a tree with leaves around,
They're twirling and dancing to the ground.
There is a tree, there is a tree,
There is a tree that is special to me.

Shona Harvey (11)
Callander Primary School, Callander

Everything is Waking

Standing in the distance
Large and round,
Was a gigantic, gloomy figure,
With roots digging into the ground.

Shimmering shadows reflecting off the light,
Seem like big, gloomy ghosties
When you see them at night.

Leaves fluttering faintly
Like beautiful ballet dancers.
See them during the dark, dreary night,
They look like the jaggy teeth of panthers.

Banging loudly, the wind is blowing!
Bumps on the tree look as if eyes are glowing.
Branches clashing together like glass plates breaking.
When I wander the woods at night,
Everything is waking.

Gemma Peebles (11)
Callander Primary School, Callander

The Chestnut Tree

The thing I remember is when me and Tom made a rope swing
And when he fell off, he didn't get hurt.
The tree was thick and brown
With yellow leaves and had some moss.

We decided to climb up the tree,
It was very high
And Tom's foot got stuck on the way down,
So I went and got my mum.

She came and we got him down.
We still play in the tree,
But we don't climb right up to the top.

Colin Hutton (11)
Callander Primary School, Callander

My Little Apple Tree

My favourite tree lives in my old back garden,
Mostly hidden by plants and flowers.
Long branches grow out of a short, stubby trunk.
A water fountain sitting underneath it.
Picking apples off my apple tree,
Making apple pies with my granny.
Round about the apples, small leaves grow.
I swing on a branch that stretches over the grass.
Bringing apples into the kitchen,
Wearing aprons that reach our toes.
When we make an apple pie, apples get chopped,
Apples as sweet as a puppy with a wagging tail.
The smell of cooking apples fills the room
As the pie cooks in the oven.
When the pie is done, I slice it up,
I eat it with ice cream and it tastes *great!*

Amy Hunter (11)
Callander Primary School, Callander

The Woods

In the woods at night,
The wind is howling,
The trees are swaying.

In the woods at night,
The leaves are rustling,
The moon is shining.

In the woods at night,
The dark is frightening,
The branches are curling.

Georgia Parkes (11)
Callander Primary School, Callander

The Cold Morning

As we walk through the cold morning woods
We see a beautiful old tree,
Tall and bold with lots of holes.
My friend climbed it and had a fall.
I climbed to the top,
How happy I was!
The river nearby is all you can hear,
Swoosh, swoosh!
Nice and quiet,
All you can hear are the birds and the river.
Leaves on the ground,
Crack! Crack! Crack!
My friend and I go home for a warm breakfast.

Scott Anderson (11)
Callander Primary School, Callander

They Brighten The World

They stay in the park,
They live in the garden.
They're covered in woody bark.
They let us live and happiness they give,
As they live in the park.

They brighten the world and with the air they have,
So we put them in wonderful gravel.
They give us paper, an assortment of things.
This is the magic that they bring.

As people fight and people play,
On the tyre swing, swing and sway.
What is it attached to, what could it be?
Our humble and loyal oak tree.

Ben Pritchard (11)
Callander Primary School, Callander

Dark And Deep

In the deep, dark wood
A lonely tree stands up tall.
Suddenly a rush of wind swoops by,
Making leaves crackle and whistle as they start to fall,
Leaving a swarm of leaves behind.

A bird starts singing,
Then tickles the leaves to make them scatter,
As he leaves, swooping through the spiky branches.

Jennifer Tait (11)
Callander Primary School, Callander

My Tree

The tree I like is in the Roman camp.
The tree is small against the other trees,
But it is still big.
I still climb it sometimes,
But when other people see me,
They come and try to push me down,
So I just jump down anyway.
Sometimes I bring a hammer to pull nails out
And then put water on it.
I climb it and friends come up
And we dare each other to jump off.

Kurt Scott (11)
Callander Primary School, Callander

The Big Tree

At the bottom of my garden lives a big tree.
Running water flows beneath for all to see.
A chestnut tree, it sways from side to side,
A lovely place for animals to hide.

Carol Martin (11)
Callander Primary School, Callander

My Favourite Tree

As the rain falls down heavily,
The tree is still standing.
I watch through the window,
The puddles are getting bigger.

The next day the sun was shining,
So I went to the tree.
It started talking,
My mum called me.
As I turned around,
The tree was still as a frozen turkey.
The tree was brown with berries,
We went to pick them,
Then *crash!*
All the leaves came falling down.
Arghhh!
I ran up the hill.
The leaves were green, yellow and orange.

The next day it grew and grew,
Up and up.
I decided to climb the tree,
So I climbed and climbed and climbed.
At last I reached the top.
My mum shouted for me,
I lost my memory.

Eilidh Allen (11)
Callander Primary School, Callander

The Conker Tree

On my tree conkers grow for me.
On the tree the bark is very lumpy,
With leaves as soft as velvet.
Conkers grow with a spiky, hard shell,
But inside lies a soft bed for conkers.

William Leckie (11)
Callander Primary School, Callander

The Golden Tree

I can see it from the bottom of the hill,
As I come closer, I see the leaves spin and fall, spin and fall.
I run upwards as leaves shout at my feet,
The wind gently cutting the leaves from the branches,
Branches failing to catch them again and again.

I'm here now looking at the scars telling me stories,
Up in the soft leaves, the midday sun filters through them.
Tiny conversations started by a single leaf sweep through the tree,
Outside the trunk looks hollow, but who knows what lies within?

Quietness wraps the tree that's too tall to climb,
Gently swaying in the breeze as the wind grows.
The leaves that rustle seem to always be wishing,
The golden-red leaves fall softly past my face,
I can almost taste the leaves, sweet like sugar,
The tree seems to be golden in the sunlight
As I walk back down the hill.

Jennifer Warnock (11)
Callander Primary School, Callander

The Snowy Tree

In the winter when the snow falls on me,
The people stop to stare at the trees filling with snow
That surround the woods I stand in.
The snow is knee-deep, but I don't sleep
Because of the soft snow that falls around me.

The woods are white for Christmas,
My friends are all in a house,
But I am still here for another year.
The forest is my home for Christmas Day,
Next year must be the time for me to leave the forest.

Alanna MacLeod (11)
Callander Primary School, Callander

The Apple Tree

I walk towards the apple tree with my basket in my hand.
First I see the tree trunk, which is thin and bumpy.
As I walk closer, I can see the dark green leaves.
I see the dark green leaves swaying in the breeze.
I'm getting closer now, I can see the bright red apples.
I pick the three biggest apples I can find
And place them in my basket.
I am happy now,
I skip back down the path,
Ready to make a delicious apple crumble.

Charlotte Hill (11)
Callander Primary School, Callander

The Repeating Tree

I stand up straight,
Up straight I stand,
I sway in the wind,
In the wind I sway,
I see the butterfly,
Flutter by me,
I see the woodpecker,
Pecking behind me,
I see the birds collecting berries,
Collect berries off me.
I've been cut down,
Cut down I've been,
But I'll grow back soon,
Soon I'll grow back.

Rebecca Davis (11)
Callander Primary School, Callander

Watching Two Squirrels Up A Tree

I was running through the woods at night,
Up the tree, two squirrels were having a fight.

The trees were swaying in the sky,
Birds were flying way up high.

A shiny river flowed through the trees,
I was stuck up the tree shouting,
'Someone help me!'

Christopher Ryan (11)
Callander Primary School, Callander

The Acorn Tree

The acorn tree is as huge as a dinosaur.
Its branches are like outstretched arms,
With fingertips scrambling to grow.
The tree grows, grows and grows,
Just the same way as water flows.
The roots are fighting for survival,
Trees are singing for Mother Earth.

Calum Foulis (11)
Callander Primary School, Callander

Walking In The Woods

As I'm walking in the woods, I'm happy.
I'm not alone, I'm with a friend,
But we're not alone, we're with trees.
These trees are whispering, but what about?
We stop by a stream to have a rest,
The wind is stinging my face as I sit on a rock.

Nicola Campbell (11)
Callander Primary School, Callander

Brown And Tall And Green

I catch my breath,
As twigs grab my back
And the wind makes leaves go scurrying.

The trees look like they're falling,
Right on top of me,
But they're not
Because they're just swaying in the breeze.

They're the giants of the forests,
They're brown and tall and green,
They live all around the world,
For everyone to see!

Fiona Wiedmann (11)
Callander Primary School, Callander

The Tunnel Tree

As we ran up that hill on Saturday night,
Up to the old tunnel tree,
Faster and faster up the steep path,
Robbie Scott and me.

We sprinted like the wind,
Only stopping now and then,
Past the hedges, the bushes and benches,
To see the tree again.

Then *crash!* We heard a noise,
We were thinking *what and where?*
We ran a little faster and faster still
And found the tree wasn't there.

Michael Ferrie (11)
Callander Primary School, Callander

What I Like About A Blossom Tree

When I see a blossom tree, I like to watch,
The leaves dancing in the breeze,
The dancing of the leaves that are twirling and fluttering by.
The feel is like smooth silk that makes you relax,
The smell is like glorious sunshine,
The colour is light growing pink,
The bark is smooth like petals from a flower.
Lovely memories float past
As I smell and feel the blossom
And that's what I like about a blossom tree.

Alicia Cowe (11)
Callander Primary School, Callander

Mother's Day

Mother, Mother
It's your day
You are special
In every way.
It's time for you
To have my love
So now I'll buy you
A great white dove.

Josh Paton (11)
Crathes Primary School, Banchory

Crathes School

Crathes School I came in P4
When Mrs Schumm opened the door
I had a little explore.
After that I couldn't wait
But now I'm leaving it's a little late.

Amy Longmore (11)
Crathes Primary School, Banchory

Loneliness

The colour of my loneliness is a colour I can't see through
A white, misty room that is more like my doom.
The taste of my loneliness is like a dry, wrinkled prune
That is being shoved into my mouth with an old, rusty spoon.
The smell of my loneliness is like a pile of old, damp socks.
When I smell this horrible smell I feel like I have chickenpox.
I cannot see my loneliness, it only makes me sad
But when my friends walk away from me,
That is when I start to get mad.
My loneliness feels . . . lonely
I am on my own, of course
I have no friends to play with
It is like I am of a different source.
My loneliness reminds me of an ant in the grass
He must be very lonely and he can't move very fast.

Christie Paterson (10)
Crown Primary School, Inverness

The Dark

Some people are haunted by the deafening screams,
By the masked murderers,
By the trickling of the streams,
But no, not I, in the never-ending hall,
I tiptoe around,
Leaving Quavers for all!

In the ebony, black night,
In the never-ending hall,
You hear a noise,
'Oh, no!' you shout,
'There is blood all . . .
Over the floor!'

Hannah Chalmers (10)
Crown Primary School, Inverness

Happiness

Happiness is yellow like the sun shining bright.
It sounds like bells ringing all through the night.
It tastes like sherbet fizzing in your mouth.
It smells like a garden full of well-kept flowers in the south.
It looks like the face of a child on Christmas Day.
It feels like the smoothest silk
Rubbing on your skin all through May.
It reminds me of laughter as children play.

Sophie Fraser (10)
Crown Primary School, Inverness

Sadness

Sadness is silver like frozen tears on my cheek,
It sounds like a slow, continuous dripping from an icicle.
It tastes like cold soup that's been left alone too long,
It smells like a salty sea, so big and trying to be brave.
It looks like a sunken ship, wrecked and ruined,
It looks like an icicle slowly dissolving as it melts away.
It reminds me of a day full of cloudy skies and fog.

Laura Jones (10)
Crown Primary School, Inverness

Happiness

Happiness is orange
It sounds like music
It tastes like a cake
It smells like freshly cut grass
It looks like a brand new Peugeot
It feels like I'm on top of the world
It reminds me of me.

Garry Maclaren (11)
Crown Primary School, Inverness

Cars

Cars, cars, some go so fast,
Cars, cars, some go so slow.
The car I'm getting I'll never be last
And hopefully I'll pass my driving test.
I will have mine green, yellow, black and blue,
Surely I'll never give it to you?
People say I'll not have enough money
But I say that that's not very funny.

Ross Whyte (9)
Crown Primary School, Inverness

Fear

Fear is red like lava
It sounds like a volcano about to explode
It tastes bitter and sour
It smells like horror
It looks like scared faces
It feels like terror
It reminds me of a volcano.

Paul Flint-Elkins (10)
Crown Primary School, Inverness

Your Fears

Fear is black like a scary, dark lane.
It sounds like darkness haunting your brain.
It tastes like beans three days old.
It smells like a car, all rusty and cold.
It looks like a fight being fought by your friend.
It feels like unhappiness that will never end.
It reminds me of my sister who drives me round the bend.

Ryan Christie (9)
Crown Primary School, Inverness

In The Sky

Freedom, freedom
Alone in the sky
All I can see is the blue shadows so bright
All I can hear is the music which helps me along
So I don't need to cry anymore
It tastes like fresh fruit picked from a tree
It smells like fresh water in the cold, winter sea
It looks like a star, so bright and spectacular
It feels like my mum, so soft and dazzling
It reminds me of what I already have.

Rebecca Maclean (10)
Crown Primary School, Inverness

Chaos, Chaos, Chaos, Chaos

Chaos is red like dark, evil eyes
It sounds like screaming and a poor child's cries
It tastes like sour sweets and mouldy old pies
It smells like gas and badly cooked fries
It looks like a ghost, a terrible surprise
It feels like mud and jelly-like eyes
It reminds me of sharks, all fierce and savage.

David Wells (10)
Crown Primary School, Inverness

Courage

Courage is green like a cliff holding up against the endless waves.
It sounds like a waterfall crashing down from above.
It smells like air in the morning sun.
It looks like a tree holding up against the vast storm.
It reminds me of a salmon struggling against the huge river.

Sam Henderson (10)
Crown Primary School, Inverness

Breakfast, Lunch And Dinner

My favourite foods are one of a kind
From brunch, spectacular bacon and eggs
To a dish called frog's legs and eggs.
The only food I won't try is none,
I find all foods enjoyable and fun.
Some people question me about my taste.
I think that is a disgrace
That some people in such a distasteful place
Could not understand the food I taste.
If you think I'm crazy,
Your mind must still be hazy
From the poem I just said
So go and have a rest
In your nice, cosy bed.

Daniel Baillie (10)
Crown Primary School, Inverness

My Pony

My pony Pippa, she's quite a show-off
Swishing her head and tail
Galloping over to me.
She loves food and loves me
And I love her.
Her colour is dapple grey
She is 13hh and her eyes shine like diamonds
Pippa reminds me of fun and laughter
When I am around her my tummy has butterflies
Because she makes me so happy
Pippa is like my best friend
I love her so much
She is the best pony in the world.

Shannon Wade (10)
Crown Primary School, Inverness

Anger!

Anger is black like a storm rushing through the dark sky
It sounds like a gunshot shooting up high
And tastes like sprouts all rotten and old.
It smells like maggots rotting in mould
And looks like a fire burning hot.
It feels hard and rough like some rocks.
It reminds me of someone drowning at the docks.

Sally Donald (10)
Crown Primary School, Inverness

Lightning!

Lightning is flashing yellow and black,
It tastes like a tooth with a little bit of plaque,
It smells like something you will never know,
It looks like lights going to and fro,
It feels like sandpaper once you are dead,
It reminds me of hate, anger and dread,
So now you know never to go out,
With lightning crashing down on your . . .
Snout!

Harry Newmark (11)
Crown Primary School, Inverness

Fun!

Fun is like a baby-blue sky in summer,
It sounds like Jingle Bells at Christmas,
It tastes like Mum's fairy cakes,
It smells like homemade lemonade,
It looks like a bunny hopping up and down,
It feels like cotton wool and
It reminds me of a pot of runny, melted chocolate.

Louise Corrigall (10)
Crown Primary School, Inverness

My Sister

My sister's name is Kelly
She's got a fat belly
She's not very tall
She's always playing with a doll.

Kelly used to be seven
But she acted like she was eleven
She is really mad but I'm just glad
That Kelly is my sister.

Nicole Petrie (10)
Crown Primary School, Inverness

How Other People See Me

To my parents I'm quite peaceful
To my brother I'm helpful and kind
To my neighbours I share things with them
To my friends I am quite caring
To my teacher I'm well behaved
But to myself I'm just me!

Allie Smeaton (8)
Douglas Primary School, Dundee

How Other People See Me

To my parents I'm a cheeky wee monkey.
To my sisters I'm a spoiled little brat.
To my brothers I'm nothing at all.
To my teacher I'm a hardworking girl
But to myself I'm just me!

Nicola Forbes (9)
Douglas Primary School, Dundee

How Other People See Me

To my parents I'm a lazy pig!
To my brother I'm horrible to him sometimes.
To my neighbours I'm the great boy next door.
To my teacher I'm a chatterbox!
But to myself I'm just me!

Aaron Ferguson (8)
Douglas Primary School, Dundee

How Other People See Me

To my parents I'm a little pest!
To my brother I'm good at toy fights.
To my neighbours I'm quiet and kind.
To my friends I share my sweets
But to myself I'm just me!

Callum Wilson (9)
Douglas Primary School, Dundee

How Other People See Me

To my parents I'm loved and cared for.
To my brother I'm the best sister.
To my neighbours I'm kind and helpful.
To my friends I share my sweets.
To my teacher I'm good at my work
But to myself I'm just me!

Reagan Kesson (8)
Douglas Primary School, Dundee

How Other People See Me

To my parents I'm a little pest!
To my brothers I'm funny!
To my neighbours I'm helpful.
To my friends I'm kind.
To my teacher I'm a little star!
But to myself I'm just me!

Courtney Ferrara (8)
Douglas Primary School, Dundee

How Other People See Me

To my parents I'm funny and kind.
To my brothers and sister I'm their world!
To my neighbours I'm very, very helpful.
To my friends I'm generous.
To my teacher I'm her pet!
But to myself I'm just me.

Melanie Martin (8)
Douglas Primary School, Dundee

How Other People See Me

To my parents I'm a pest!
To my sister I'm a silly boy!
To my next door neighbours I'm kind!
To my friends I'm helpful!
To my teacher I'm a star!
But to myself I'm just me!

Aaron Quinn (8)
Douglas Primary School, Dundee

How Other People See Me

To my parents I'm a cheeky boy!
To my brother/sister I'm a brat!
To my neighbour I'm a chatterbox.
To my friends I'm the best.
To my teacher I'm a brilliant worker
But to myself I'm just me!

Darren Young (8)
Douglas Primary School, Dundee

What Summer Means To Me

Superb strawberry ice cream
Relaxing in the sun - *yawn!*
Having a barbecue - yummy!
Playing with my friends.
Going places - *great!*
Having long lie-ins.

Jemma Sproull (8)
Douglas Primary School, Dundee

Summer Is . . .

Beautiful butterflies fluttering among the flowers.
A long-haired Jack Russell panting in the heat.
Sizzling burgers on the barbecue.
Freezing ice lolly sticking on my tongue.
The nice, smooth sand on my toes.

Nathan-Lee Brown (9)
Douglas Primary School, Dundee

Summer Is . . .

Pretty butterflies fluttering in the sky.
Bees buzzing round the garden.
Burnt sausages on the smoky barbecue.
Hot burgers that are on your plate.
The golden sand on the hot beach.

Lori Doreen Allan (9)
Douglas Primary School, Dundee

Summer Is . . .

Children playing in the pale blue water
Hot barbecues smoking and sizzling
The fresh, deep blue sea
Eating cold ice cream cones
Smooth and jagged shells.

Danielle Crawford (9)
Douglas Primary School, Dundee

Firework - Haiku

Fireworks exploding
Shooting around the night sky
Silver, gold and green.

Jamie Lowrey (9)
Douglas Primary School, Dundee

Firework - Haiku

Loud, banging fireworks,
Exploding in the dark sky,
Burning bonfires too.

Michelle Donnelly (10)
Douglas Primary School, Dundee

Harvest

I see little, brown mice running about mad in the fields
When the farmer cuts down the corn.
I see a lot of fruit and vegetables in the shops.
I hear hedgehogs snuffling in the leaves.
I hear children playing in the leaves.
I smell smoke in the garden
When people are burning their rubbish.
I touch the smooth conkers that have been blown off the trees.
I taste a cup of soup when it's cold at night.

Chloe Anderson (9)
Douglas Primary School, Dundee

How Other People See Me

To my parents I'm spoilt and ruined!
To my brother and sister I'm a nutcase and a maniac!
To my neighbours I'm a great friend!
To my friends I'm really funny and goofy!
To my teacher I'm a great artist!
But to myself I'm just me!

Sally Robertson (8)
Douglas Primary School, Dundee

Harvest

I see the farmers harvesting their crops
I hear whistling wind
And crusty leaves being blown along the ground
I smell the newly-cut grass in the park
I touch the red, juicy berries on the branches
I taste the juicy pumpkin with my carrots.

Gavin Lee Thomson (9)
Douglas Primary School, Dundee

How Other People See Me

To my parents I am a nice girl.
To my auntie I'm loving.
To my neighbours I'm good to them.
To my friends I'm kind.
To my teacher I'm a star!
But to myself I'm just me!

Sarah Murphy (8)
Douglas Primary School, Dundee

The Commentator

And Shauni is stroking her teeth,
Yes and her hand is going in,
And is that her thumb?
Yes! Oh golly, she is sucking her thumb!
Oh wow! This has never been seen before.
What is she doing now?
Her finger is on her chin,
She is thinking.
Is her hand going up? Is it?
Oh no, it went down.
She's thinking again.
Her hand is on her face
And, and
Her hand's up
And she is giving a fabulous answer.
Now she's getting up,
She's getting a book.
Oh, she's talking
And the teacher looks around
And she stops talking
And she's making a run for her seat
And *goal!*
She makes it back just in time!

Sophie McDonald (11)
Downfield Primary School, Dundee

School

Going into this horrible place
And seeing the teacher's ugly face
My parents say it's a great place
But they don't know what goes on
In this school

Parents don't know about the teacher's whip
Or the cane's pointed tip
The playground is an evil space
People that are in this place
It's a barbaric race

The food is fit for a dog
And the dinner ladies look like hogs
The toilets have a horrible smell
A smell that is too horrible to tell
Never go near this hell

We are worked to the bone
Children never dare to moan
Or we will be put in the rubbish bin
If you think you know school
Think again . . .

Ricky Warden (11)
Downfield Primary School, Dundee

Moonlight

Moonlight creeps across the sky,
Slow, as though it's shy,
Casting silver light all over the land.
Glittering and sparkling like little grains of sand.
It lovingly spreads a gleaming white light,
Like a motherly feature that comes out at night.
The rays of light touch the darkest fears,
To make sure they are nowhere near.
When the moon goes home,
She leaves all the people alone.

Leeann Chen (9)
Downfield Primary School, Dundee

A Story At Night

My dad told a story about a monster
That made me think he was not really but . . .
When I looked under the bed
I saw an alien head.
I tried to get to sleep
But all I could hear were creaks and stomps.
I peeked my eye open,
Got out of bed,
Looked in my shoe,
I saw poo.
I looked in my wardrobe behind clothes,
I saw the alien strike a pose.
I screamed!
Quick!
Under
The covers!

Kayleigh McDermott (11)
Downfield Primary School, Dundee

Through That Door . . .

Through that door,
Is a golden palace with magnificent gardens and statues,
I can smell the faint scent of flowers,
I feel a small, cool breeze on my face,
I feel very joyful.

Through that door,
Is where everyone dreams of and hopes to go,
But this world feels so real,
Yet it is really made of images and is an illusion.

Through that door,
I can hear my name being called in a bewitching song
But I know this isn't real.

Ryan Peet (11)
Downfield Primary School, Dundee

The Panda's Owner

There once was a panda
Whose owner Amanda
Decided to go away
But soon she was back with a gigantic sack
Filled to the top with hay.

The very next day stood
A large heap of wood
It lay by the dark red gate
Amanda built a stable
It was steady and tall
And put up at quite a rate.

Panda got a big surprise
To see a pony soon arrive
They played and played
All through the day.

Amanda was happy to see panda and pony go in for tea
She hoped they'd be the best of friends
And she would love them 'til the end.

Megan Connor (9)
Downfield Primary School, Dundee

A Lady From Prague

There once was an old lady from Prague,
Who was an ancient hag,
She ate some sunflower seeds,
And began to weed,
All over her bald head.
Sunflowers grew to the size of her bed,
An eager fashion designer stopped her in the street,
They talked a lot, anxious again to meet.
Three months later the word was out,
Every five minutes she got a shout,
Because she was famous she started to mock
And then she appeared on the catwalk!

Hayley MacFarlane (11)
Downfield Primary School, Dundee

10 Things You'll Find In Your Childminder's House

Under the beds you'll find some heads.
Behind the drawers there are skeletons.
On the kitchen table there's a book to cook kids
And bottles of poison, baskets of bodies
And worst of all in the cellar . . .
There's a velociraptor,
A pile of man-eating bugs and coffins of spikes,
A pool of piranhas and a bloodthirsty bat.

Adam Hindmarch (10)
Downfield Primary School, Dundee

Kangaroos

Do you know that kangaroos
Kick high and bounce quite low
At night in the outback
They bounce to and fro.

The baby kangaroo
Joey is his name
Kicks high and bounces low
To him it's just a game.

Benn Cooper (10)
Downfield Primary School, Dundee

To My Valentine

My Valentine is cute
He wears a very smart suit
I also want to kiss him
But I'm scared in case I miss him
When he goes away.

Terri Skelligan (9)
Downfield Primary School, Dundee

Springtime

The sky is blue, the grass is green
The trees are tall, their branches lean.
With beautiful colours of brown and green,
Spring is nearly here.
The birds are singing in the trees
Beautiful songs for us to hear.
Winter is nearly at an end
And spring will soon be here.
The beautiful flowers have started to bloom
The snow has melted
The river flows
Now you know it is time for winter to go
'Cause spring is here.

Stephanie McDonald (9)
Downfield Primary School, Dundee

10 Things You'll Find In A Teacher's House

You'll find a headless chicken running around,
A secret door leading underground,
You'll find that teachers love to eat pie,
And that is why
They cannot fly.

You'll find a great big, hairy dog,
A skeleton who's been hit by a log,
A recipe book of 'How To Cook Kids',
You find a basement full of lids,
A hand that's missing a finger and thumb,
But worst of all the teacher's my mum!

Sam Hill (10)
Downfield Primary School, Dundee

Through That Door . . .

Through that door,
Was my bed,
With huge, fuzzy pillows,
And sweltering covers,
I see the heat waves coming up.

Through that door,
Are lots of animals,
One lion with a furry mane,
A tiger licked my hands,
And the noise was like a thunderstorm.

Through that door,
Jogging out of a massive tunnel at dens,
A brilliant smell of burgers from the stands,
Where echoing wouldn't stop,
I felt great.

Jordan Carrie (10)
Downfield Primary School, Dundee

A Strange Journey

'Where are you going, little laddie?'
'Out with my dog, Mr McPaddie,
I'm going to sea
To be free,
Would you like to come with me, Daddy?'

When we went we met a little cat
He said he was the cat in the hat
He sat on my knee
Then set off for Dundee
He did a little dance on the mat.

Danielle Hunter (10)
Downfield Primary School, Dundee

Lost Things

Oh bother!
I've lost my wand again!

Maybe it's behind the shed.
No, but here's that potion I've been looking for . . .
I'll put it in my potions chest.

Oh! Here's that cauldron I've been looking for . . .
I'll put it beside the washing machine.
Oh! Here's that hat I've been looking for . . .
I'll put it under my bed.
Oh! Here's that toilet seat I've been looking for . . .
I'll put it on my coat peg.
Oh! Here's that owl cage I've been looking for . . .
I'll put it behind the wardrobe.
Oh! Here's that magical book I've been looking for . . .
I'll put it in front of the toilet.
Oh! Here are those pyjamas I've been looking for . . .
I'll put them in my cloak pocket.
Oh! Here's my wand! *Hooray!*

Now, where did I put my glasses . . . ?

Ashleigh Nicoll (10)
Downfield Primary School, Dundee

10 Things In A Dragon's Pocket

10 things in a dragon's pocket are . . .
A big, white rat for tea
A tablet to make him see
A little baby goat
A big, blue coat
A giant bee
A rusty key
A boy called Lee
A monster's knee
A man-eating pea
And me - *gee!*

Celena Caswell (9)
Downfield Primary School, Dundee

The Hamster

There was once a hamster, his name was Prancer
He was very small and cute
The only thing he liked to do
Was to play his wee blue flute.

One day I asked Prancer
If he'd like to be a dancer,
He replied, 'Toot, toot, toot!'
Then he danced a little jig
As he played on his wee blue flute.

Anil Findlay (9)
Downfield Primary School, Dundee

Rain

The farmer's horse was reining up,
The rain was raining down,
The king was reigning over all,
The country and the town,
They reined and rained and reigned together,
And that was surely April weather.

Jordan Noon (10)
Downfield Primary School, Dundee

The Brazilian

There once was a man from Brazil
Who swallowed an explosive pill
Arms and legs squashed like fried eggs
His head falling through his bed
And his heart rolled down the hill.

Ross McCormack (11)
Downfield Primary School, Dundee

Cats And Dogs

Oh cats and dogs,
What are they like?
The cat's called Felix
And the dog's Spike,
Never get a moment's peace,
Well, never can in my life.

The chair belongs to the cat,
The bed belongs to the dog,
And surprisingly, the floor belongs to me,
I'm the servant
That comes when they ring the bell,
The dog rests its ears
And the cat rests its tail.

I do this and that,
I clean things out,
I would love to get out,
Oh yes!
I never get a minute's rest,
But I love them both
The very best!

Oh cats and dogs,
What are they like?
The cat's called Felix,
And the dog's Spike.

Sian Cochrane (10)
Downfield Primary School, Dundee

Soccer

S is for our home nation, Scotland,
O is for all the own goals,
C is for the best team, Celtic,
C is our great player, Camara,
E is for Ellington who we need to sign,
R is our biggest rivals, Rangers.

Liam McDonald (11)
Downfield Primary School, Dundee

Supersonic

Supersonic with your eyes so blue,
You whiz about like you've got the flu,
Kicking and jumping with such flare,
You better watch you don't fall down the stair.
You fight aliens, monsters and robots,
You're so fast it's hard to believe
That you don't run out of steam.
You're so fast I think you're daft,
My mum laughed with her draft.
She'd daft, Sonic, you're my hero.
Your mum and dad must be proud
Because they're so loud.
I'm just proud.
My dad thinks you're so cool,
Like my pool,
But you're more cool
Because you're just full of fuel.

Beth Clark (9)
Downfield Primary School, Dundee

Through That Door . . .

Through that door is an ancient boat
And I can smell the ocean water
And I hear the sound
And I hear the sound of the waves hitting the bow.

Through that door I see a giant swimming pool
And the sight of the sky-blue water
And you can hear the splashing of children playing.

Connor Hutt (11)
Downfield Primary School, Dundee

That Girl

There was a girl, she had no name,
No one knew her quite the same.
That girl, she walks alone
No one told her, 'Dry your eyes.'
She looked at the starry skies.
That girl she walks alone
As the trees began to swing
And the wind
Began to roar.
That girl, she walks alone.
That girl, she had no family.
She never goes to sleep at night.
That girl, she disappears.
No one noticed.
They did not care.
And that girl
She will remain as the girl, she walks alone.

Amy Wilcox (9)
Downfield Primary School, Dundee

The Sunset

The sunset is pink and red,
I watch it before I go to bed,
I think of lovely things in my head,
The sunset is pink and red.

I invited my friends to see it,
Then they fell asleep,
So I had to creep,
Oh the sunset is a lovely thing,
It just makes you want to sing.

Shauni Leigh Griffiths (11)
Downfield Primary School, Dundee

A Little Girl

When Gran was a little girl
They didn't have lots of money
But one treat that they used to get
Was a little drop of honey

Milk was scarce and sugar too
And juice, they didn't have any
But when Dad came home on Friday night
He gave them each a penny

She used to make homemade bread
And little biscuits too
'Cos everything was in short supply
And it was rationed too

But now she says those days have gone
And her cupboards are always full
And thinks about those days long ago
When she was a little girl

But now she's glad those days are gone
That's how it used to be
I'm glad I wasn't born then
I'm glad I am just me.

Beth Jowett (9)
Downfield Primary School, Dundee

Mondays And Fridays

Monday morning, worst day ever,
Friday afternoon can't get better.
Go to the baker's on Friday for lunch,
Back to school for quarter-past one.

Golden time is after break,
The music room keeps you awake.
We have an hour from half-past two,
Our classroom ends up like a zoo!

Shaunni Pollock (11)
Downfield Primary School, Dundee

Magic Spell

Hubble bubble, toil and trouble
Eye of newt
And fungi root
I'll make a potion
And I'll turn you into a toad

Hubble bubble, toil and trouble
Wing of bat
And tail of cat
I'll turn you into a snake

Hubble bubble, toil and trouble
I'll turn you good
Fairies, pixies
And wormwood
I command you to be good.

Jack Harris (10)
Downfield Primary School, Dundee

The School

Warm and welcoming,
Yeah, right!
That's what they make you think.
It's fight after fight,
And the toilets *stink!*
The bell starts to ring
Oh no! School's about to begin.
They pull you inside and lock you in,
They hardly ever turn their back.
No matter what, they always win,
So you dare slack.
What are these terrible creatures?
Well, these things are called
Teachers!

Rachel Tardito (11)
Downfield Primary School, Dundee

Through That Door . . .

Through that door
I see the pitch-black, dirty water
Tearing down the bank like an avalanche
Mummies floating down the gorge
With only half their bandages left.

Through that door
I hear witches singing and casting evil spells
On lifeless people's gravestones
And they are laughing like a screeching cat
In the creepy graveyard.

Through that door
Canada is waiting for me
Where hockey is everything
And the theme parks are magic
Where I could touch Niagara Falls.

Scott McRae (10)
Downfield Primary School, Dundee

What An Adventure!

There once was a man from Dundee
Who bought a book from Discovery Quay
He ran to Paisley
And lost his way
So he decided to swim in the sea

The man from Dundee
Returned to Discovery Quay
He got out of the water
And spotted an otter
That was on its way to Lochee.

Becky Polson (10)
Downfield Primary School, Dundee

The Playground

The girls gossiping,
The boys playing football.
The primary ones running round like crazy!
Some of the girls upset
Because they've fallen out with their friends,
Some of them angry
Because their friends have spoke about them.
It's, 'She said this, she said that,'
Why can't it all just stop?
Though if you think the girls are bad,
Check out the boys
'Cause here's what it's like . . .
'It's a goal!'
'That wissna in!'
'Yeah, it was!'
'Mon then!'
You wouldn't believe it was like that, would you?
Just a simple game of football
But it is, I've played and it gets more violent,
Mind you, it's just a playground after all!

Brogan Webster (11)
Downfield Primary School, Dundee

School Bag

I cleaned my school bag out
When I found . . .
Letters from last year
2 broken pencils
A cucumber sandwich
Smelly gym socks
Ripped up jotters
And a mouldy, rotten apple.

Now I have a clean bag
But Mum still doesn't go in there!

Dale Robertson (9)
Downfield Primary School, Dundee

Through That Door . . .

Through that door,
I see a garden with pink and purple flowers,
With a clear, sparkling river,
With golden fish in it,
And it is garden heaven.

Through that door,
Is a waterfall which shimmers day and night,
With all the fishes swimming in and out,
While the sun is fluttering down.

Through that door,
I see the shooting stars,
Glittering all over the dark blue sky,
Where all the beautiful planets sit quietly.

Sarah Fleck (11)
Downfield Primary School, Dundee

Through That Door . . .

Through that door
I see the biggest football stadium in Europe,
The fans are cheering like a million bears,
As I run on to the pitch,
My best friends are in the stands.

Through that door
I have the football at my feet
I tap it down the middle to Ronaldinho
A defender tackles him
And it's a free kick!

Through that door
I put the ball down
I smell victory is one kick away
I run up and shoot, it curves round the wall
The back of the net . . . *goal!*

Peter Hine (11)
Downfield Primary School, Dundee

Classroom Alphabet

A is for the alphabet that sits on the wall
B is for the blackboard we don't use at all
C is for the cupboard broken down last week
D is for the door that makes a squeak
E is for the electricity we never touch
F is for the football that boys like so much
G is for the genius that works very hard
H is for the head teacher that plays with a card
I is for the ink that always spills
J is for the job where you get the bills
K is for the kids that always talk
L is for the lessons where the teachers use chalk
M is for the mental Maths where I'm never stuck
N is for the nickname which brings me good luck
O is for the object that sits on my table
P is for the pencil which has a label
Q is for the quiet class which never is true
R is for the ruler which gets covered in glue
S is for the sausage which we have at lunch
T is for the tango where we go *crunch, crunch*
U is for the umbrella when it rains
V is for the vegetable which gives me pains
W is for the wasp that goes *buzz, buzz, buzz*
X is for the xylophone which sometimes is a fuzz
Y is for the yellow paint which goes *splash, splash*
Z is for the zooming kids trying to steal the cash.

Ashleigh Roberts (11)
Downfield Primary School, Dundee

Red

When the sun rises in the month of May,
Red jumps out to start a new day.
It can remind people of their ills,
Or when they have to pay the bills.
Red has emotions, feelings and pain,
No other colour inspires the same.

When you are hurt I'm sure you will find,
Red is the colour that comes into mind.
It's the colour of love,
Like the grace of a sweet dove.
Red is the colour that sets me free,
It is the colour most important to me.

Thomas Taylor (11)
Drakies Primary School, Inverness

White!

The white, white feathers,
In the white, white pillow,
In the white, white room,
Of the white, white house,
In the white, white field,
And the white, white snow,
Covers white, white snowdrops,
And some white, white snowflakes,
Fall from white, white clouds,
Where there's the white, white Heaven,
And some white, white angels,
Play with white, white doves,
That soar in the blue, blue sky!

Robyn Stark (11)
Drakies Primary School, Inverness

Colours Are Great, Colours Are Wonderful

White is for peace,
To wave the white flag.
Black is for darkness,
Evil and bad.
Yellow is for happiness,
A smiling face.
Green is for life,
Like the human race.
Blue is for the sea,
Where seagulls fly low.
Brown is for the mountains,
Tipped with snow.
Red is for danger,
Get up and run.
Pink is for beauty,
A pink-topped bun.
All the colours of the rainbow,
Are just so great.
The colours of the rainbow,
Are worth the wait.

Adam Kelly (11)
Drakies Primary School, Inverness

White

White is like snow,
Snow like the doves,
Doves like the clouds,
Clouds like Heaven.
Heaven soft and white as pillows,
Pillows like angels,
Angels with doves,
All memories of last night's dream.

Gemma Ross (11)
Drakies Primary School, Inverness

White

White is a colour that makes me think,
Of peace and calmness and their link.
It's the sight of snowdrops sprouting in the spring,
And the voice of the robin as I listen to him sing.
It's the blast you get from the fresh, winter air,
And the rough feeling of my collie dog's hair.
It's the colour I go when I'm really scared or hurt,
It's the cleanest feeling - it repels all dirt.
It's up in the mountains, way up high,
In the tranquil dove as it flies by.
White may seem a plain colour to choose,
But its emptiness tells me I have nothing to lose.

Stacey MacDonald (11)
Drakies Primary School, Inverness

Sports Day

I'm nervous, I'm scared
At the starting line,
It's alright, don't worry
I'll be just fine.

I'm winning, I'm winning!
My mum will be so proud.
I probably think so
From the cheer of the crowd!

I've won, I've won!
I knew I'd be fine.
The sweet smell of victory
Is finally mine!

Jake Mackenzie (11)
Drakies Primary School, Inverness

The Sandy Surf

I can feel the sand between my toes,
As the people get into their swimming clothes!

The blue sky and the silky-smooth seaweed,
Glitter as the seagulls beg for a feed!

People playing in the great big sea,
As the warmth goes up degree by degree!

It's getting cold, you're about to leave,
You turn around and you start to grieve,
'I don't want to go, I want to stay,
Will we come back another day?'

Lesley Barron (11)
Drakies Primary School, Inverness

The Beach

Walking down the beach
Hearing children screech
The sound of the waves
Crashing and bashing.

The birds flying everywhere
The sand blowing in the air
The sun's in my face
As I look up into space.

People jumping into the sea
People bumping into me
The day is bright
With so much light.

Oh I love these summer days.
Oh I wish they were with me always.

Sarah Baxter (11)
Drakies Primary School, Inverness

Canaries

Canaries like to sing
They sing and sing
Canaries like to sing and cheep
They cheep and sing and sing and cheep.

Canaries like to flutter about
They flutter about without a doubt
Canaries like to eat some seed
They can eat it because it is their feed.

David Richard Mckinney (9)
Dunblane Primary School, Dunblane

Teachers

Teachers are creatures
They live in the school
Most of them are strict
But some of them are cool
They're not always fun
They want work to be done
Teachers are creatures
And they live in the school.

Toby Goodwin (9)
Dunblane Primary School, Dunblane

Piranhas

Piranhas snapping everywhere,
Don't you dare move anywhere,
If you do I'll go on a crew
And leave you for fish stew,
They bite your hands,
They cannot stand
And they do not play in a band.

Mark Ryan (9)
Dunblane Primary School, Dunblane

The Last Rose Of Summer

It's the last day of summer
And I'm lying in my bed,
I'm thinking about the roses
Going away.

When it's the morning
I run away outside,
I see something incredible,
'I'm dreaming,' I said.

While summer goes out
And autumn comes in,
I'm standing there stunned
With nothing to say.

It was the last rose of summer,
I shout to my mum, 'Get out here!'
She comes out worried and I say,
'It's the last rose of summer, OK?'

Johanna Elizabeth Martin (9)
Dunblane Primary School, Dunblane

Cats

Cats like playing with string
Isn't that a strange thing?
Cats like to sleep all day
They also like to play.

Cats like drinking milk
They like to cuddle in your quilt
Cats like chasing mice
They think they taste nice.

Cats like to nose about
Until they hear you shout
Cats like to chase your feet
And all the people that they meet.

Hayley Louise Aleix Robb (9)
Dunblane Primary School, Dunblane

This Sucks!

This sucks!
Off to school again,
I tried skiving with a sore throat,
But it never works.

This sucks!
Off to the shops again,
I wanted a day off (for once),
It always happens.

This sucks!
Banned from the computer again,
I wanted to play Dark Evil,
But it's an 18.

This doesn't suck!
Off to the sweet shop for once,
I love you, Mum!

Grant Lawrie (9)
Dunblane Primary School, Dunblane

Dogs

Dogs like playing with bones,
They like digging up stones,
Dogs like going for walks,
They like chewing socks.

Dogs like eating bones,
They always bring back stones,
Dogs like to keep warm,
Their blankets are always torn.

Dogs like drinking water,
Even if it was a little bit hotter,
Dogs like to go for a swim,
And I always go after him.

Craig Symon (9)
Dunblane Primary School, Dunblane

Pets

Dogs are big, dogs are scary,
Dogs will eat your canaries.
Some dogs are as big as hogs,
That's why some people like dogs.

Cats, cats are much bigger than bats,
Sometimes posh cats wear hats.
Cats can run faster than me,
Sometimes they're even faster than a Ferrari.

Mice, mice like to nibble rice,
And they sometimes eat oriental spice.
They're kind of small,
Hey, but that doesn't mean they can't be tall!

Andrew McCulloch (9)
Dunblane Primary School, Dunblane

The Snake

A snake likes to cuddle you
And it likes to strangle you.
A snake is a lovely thing
But it can't do the right thing.
Why does it kill you?
Why can't it live with you?
We welcome you to the Snake Hotel
Where he can live and tell.
Now we have got rid of the snake
We can have great milkshake
And the snake, so we say,
Loved to slither and play.

Ryan Anderson (9)
Dunblane Primary School, Dunblane

Little Car

A little car, a little car
A little car is what I saw
It honked its horn
And started its engine
And, *'Peep, peep!'*
It said to me
Peep-peeped me
Goodbye.

Wesley Wright (9)
Dunblane Primary School, Dunblane

A Man Called Paddy

There once was a man called Paddy,
Who had a very big daddy,
He went to the attack
And broke his back
That was the end of Paddy.

Victoria Anne Sutherland (9)
Dunblane Primary School, Dunblane

I'd Love To Be A Caterpillar

I'd love to be a caterpillar
So hairy and so round
I'd be so happy and I'll never have to frown
I'd probably get a reward
I'd love to be a caterpillar.

Sean Brown (9)
Dunblane Primary School, Dunblane

The Food Fight

It all started on a normal day,
I was working at school on the first of May,
When all of a sudden,
It all broke out,
The grand, grand food fight of Grout.
There was food flying all around,
On the carpet,
In a mound,
On the tables,
On the chairs,
It was coming out in food flairs.
There were people with spaghetti lassos
And people throwing cakes with their shoes,
But I had a pizza rifle,
Except soon on my face I had a trifle.
I quickly licked it off my face,
Mmmm, I thought, *this tastes great!*
Then I grabbed a chocolate sword,
And hit someone hard enough to put them in a ward.
But it didn't hurt one bit,
He just munched it up
And called me an it.
Then someone caught me with their spaghetti,
They pulled it round, round and around,
I said, 'Stop and I'll give you a pound.'
Now it was all up to me,
I threw a cake at the teacher,
He went really, really mad,
He said, *'Stop it now! It is getting bad!'*

Anthony Jones (10)
Dunblane Primary School, Dunblane

My Doggy

My dog is cool,
Better than the rest,
My dog makes up dances
And does tricks.

My dog even watches TV
And I forgot to tell you
He is very lazy
All the kids in the street
Come to my house
Just to see my dog.

My dog is the best!

Jill Rowan (9)
Dunblane Primary School, Dunblane

Bunnies

Bunnies jumping
Through the air.
They don't care.
Jumping here.
Jumping there.
Everywhere.
Munching carrots
With their strong teeth.
Twitching noses
To everyone they meet.

Eilidh McIntosh (9)
Dunblane Primary School, Dunblane

My Doggy

My doggy is the best doggy in the world.
Everyone likes him and pats him.
When I am hurt he comes to my rescue
Then I try to thank him.
He bites me
So I shout at him, 'Naughty!'
So he growls at me
And pounces on me
And we get into a big fight
And it all ends up in tears.
If you're wondering whose tears
They were his!

Erin Campbell (9)
Dunblane Primary School, Dunblane

Sam

There was a tiny boy.
One day he came up to me and he said,
'Hi, I'm Sam, the invisible man.'
'But I can see you.'
'No you can't!'
Said Sam, the invisible man.
'Where do you live?'
'In my invisible van.'

Anna Skinner (9)
Dunblane Primary School, Dunblane

The Witch

There was an old witch called Bubble
She was making a spell with trouble
She was having lots of fun with her new spell
But she got in a bit of a muddle.
Bubble! Bubble! Bubble!

Andrew Howie (9)
Dunblane Primary School, Dunblane

Pancakes

Pancakes flip,
Pancakes fly,
Pancakes even say goodbye.

Pancakes twirl,
Pancakes whirl,
Pancakes even sometimes furl.

Pancakes dance,
Pancakes prance,
Pancakes even say their thanks.

Pancakes sizzle,
Pancakes fry,
Pancakes even make me sigh.

Megan Kate Priestley (9)
Dunblane Primary School, Dunblane

School

School I hate
But my mate thinks it's great
I am always late
I get shouted at
Just because I am smart
And I know the 8 times table
Off by heart
We always sing
It's not very bling
The teacher's mad
And very sad
And that's the poem
That I had.

Awais Bhatti (9)
Dunblane Primary School, Dunblane

Animals

Fish swim
Here and there
Fish swim
Everywhere

Dolphins jump
Here and there
Dolphins jump
Everywhere

Cats sleep
Here and there
Cats sleep
Everywhere

Dogs run
Here and there
Dogs run
Everywhere

Horses canter
Here and there
Horses canter
Everywhere

Rabbits eat
Here and there
Rabbits eat
Everywhere

Monkeys swing
Here and there
Monkeys swing
Everywhere.

Georgina Mountford (9)
Dunblane Primary School, Dunblane

Playground Bell

Ten o'clock
Ten o'clock playground bell
Everybody hurrying
Out of school

Out to the playground
They do run
Out to play
And have fun

When the bell rings again
Time to go inside
Go and do work
And wait for the next bell.

Kerry Jane Anderson (9)
Dunblane Primary School, Dunblane

Dogs

Dogs jump anywhere
On a table, on a chair
They don't care
They will jump anywhere

Dogs dig holes anywhere
In the garden, anywhere
They find stones in their holes
Not just stones but bones

Dogs pick up sticks
Sometimes even six
They mix stones in with sticks
And they're always full of tricks.

Jordan Grant Wilson (9)
Dunblane Primary School, Dunblane

Hallowe'en Night

H orrible ghosts
A nd horrible witches
L ots of children
L ooking for riches
O pportunity knocks
W hen the door is open
E veryone laughing and
E veryone joking
N ice to see everyone having fun.

Jodie Malley (9)
Dunblane Primary School, Dunblane

Monkeys

Monkeys come from
Different places,
They like going
In rainforest races,
They like swinging
In the trees,
And humming with
The humming bees.

Nicola Robertson (9)
Dunblane Primary School, Dunblane

Bullying

Bullying, bullying everywhere,
In the playground
And on the stair.
Bullying, bullying is not nice.
Bullying, bullying is making someone cry.
Bullying, bullying is just like
Breaking someone's heart.

Emma Crosbie (9)
Dunblane Primary School, Dunblane

I'm Too Cool For School!

School shmule, I'm too cool for school
'Cause I rule, I'm ultra, mega cool
I just like chillin' in my pool
Keepin' nice and cool
Whoever goes to school
Is a big, fat fool
'Cause I rule, I'm super, duper cool
My mum usually says,
You go to school for education,
Yeah, right,
I just sit in my chair
Doin' my hair,
I don't act the fool
'Cause I don't go to school
I rule, I have millions of cash,
I have a great big stash
I'm super, duper, ultra, mega cool
I rule
'Cause I'm cool
Yeah!

Ryan Hornby (9)
Dunblane Primary School, Dunblane

Fish

I have a fish,
Who lives in a dish,
Her name is Shimmer,
Who doesn't get thinner,
She swims around with the plants,
And does a little dance,
She doesn't have a mum or dad,
Which makes her very mad,
I never feed her bread,
Because now she is dead.

Catriona McDonald (9)
Dunblane Primary School, Dunblane

My Debut

I came walking down the tunnel
As nervous as could be
We started to have a kick about
Jamie, Sam and me
And then we were called together
Because it was huddle time
We had to plan our strategy
We were going to win this time
We had to beat them - Rangers
But they wanted to win too
And then we kicked and hit
The bar before half time
We got a fifteen minute break
And it was a good thing too
Because my poor legs started to ache
But then I came back on and scored
And then the whistle blew
And I thought, *that was a perfect way*
To have play my debut.

Conor McDonald Beaton (9)
Dunblane Primary School, Dunblane

Dogs

Dogs sleep
Anywhere
In their bed
On the couch
In the middle
Of the floor
Top of someone's bed
Someone's lap
They don't care
So that's dogs
For you.

Cameron Christmas (9)
Dunblane Primary School, Dunblane

My Grandma Rode On A Tiger

My grandma rode on a tiger,
She did, she did, she did,
My grandma rode on a tiger,
She did it in Madrid.

But when we opened the door,
It was not Grandma,
But a tiger on the floor,
It spoke with Grandma's tone,
It sounded like her speaking on the phone.

For when I have to feed her,
I feed a tiger instead,
And she has to share my bed,
It's really strange to me,
That I have a tiger for a grandma,
That likes to share my tea.

Catherine Wilson (9)
Dunblane Primary School, Dunblane

Pigs

There are lots of pigs
Big ones, fat ones
Sometimes you get a pig in a wig
Pigs never run
They always snore
The pigs rub in the mud
They have a big, big nose
That is as pink as a rose
All they say is, *'Oink, oink, oink!'*
Also they are pink
But most of all they stink!

Erin McLagan (9)
Dunblane Primary School, Dunblane

Gymnastics

I like to go to gymnastics,
It's really wicked and fun.
For our warm-up we run around the hall
Gymnastics is wickedly fun.

I like to swirl and twirl around,
But some old, boring people . . .
Just sit on the ground.
If you come twice
You have to be nice,
Gymnastics is wickedly fun.

So now I have told you about what I love,
My work is done,
I hope you can come,
So now time for some fun!

Fiona Brown (9)
Dunblane Primary School, Dunblane

Vegetables

Dad, I hate vegetables
They're green and sweet.
I think that they're sour
But I get told off
For saying that.
Last night
At dinner
We had to have peas.
I can't eat it!
Mmmm, they're delicious.

Grant Groat (9)
Dunblane Primary School, Dunblane

My Packed Lunch

My packed lunch has its own wee bunch
With sweets, doughnuts and more.
There's fruit gums and ice cream
Fizzy lemonade with strawberries
And cream and even chicken soup.
Pizza, yummy, for my lips
And even fish and chips.
There was no chocolate milkshake
But I had a creamy, creamy cake.
I had a good packed lunch
So what's for dinner now?

Gordon Davison (9)
Dunblane Primary School, Dunblane

Foals

Foals prance,
Here and there,
In the stable,
Through the air.

Foals eat some hay,
From the net nearby,
To make them strong,
As the day goes by.

Foals will grow big,
Into a horse,
They will have power,
And pull with force.

Jennifer Ross (9)
Dunblane Primary School, Dunblane

My Family

When my mummy goes to town,
She visits all the shops,
The ice cream bar,
The book shop,
The jewellery shop,
The lot!

When my dad has a bath,
He takes so long too,
Uses all the bubble bath
And warm water too!

But I'm perfect,
'Cos I don't take too long in the bath,
I don't visit all the shops
Or use all the bubble bath!

Eilidh Wilson (9)
Dunblane Primary School, Dunblane

Dog

The shadow in the park
I wonder what it is
Let's go and see
The silent swings
I wonder what it is?
Is that a hissing sound?
Is it a cat?
I don't think it is a cat by the gate
A barking sound by the bush
I remember
It is just my dad's new dog.

Christopher Smith (9)
Dunblane Primary School, Dunblane

You're Not Going Out Like That!

'You're not going out like that!
You're not going with nothing on!
You're not going with a bikini on!
You're not going out with a swimsuit on!
You're not going out like that!
Put your trousers and cool top on.'
'But that is boring.'
'Well, you're not going out like that!'

Alice Stewart (9)
Dunblane Primary School, Dunblane

Clash With The Titans

Today I will clash with the titans
They come in many shapes and sizes
And are all there for one reason
To make us learn a lesson
And now I fear the worst
For it is parents' night.

Robin Lee (9)
Dunblane Primary School, Dunblane

Camp

I hate camp,
I hate the cold toast at camp,
The breakfast is disgusting,
I hate getting dirty at camp,
When I have no spare clothes.
I only go to camp because
I like sleeping on bunk beds.

Neil Groat (9)
Dunblane Primary School, Dunblane

Big Brothers

Big brothers are silly
Strange and
Annoying
The problem with big brothers is
They're like a big machine
They always win the match
But when they start a fight
Guess who gets in trouble? *Me!*
They get to watch 15s
When you settle with a PG
They get to eat big dinners
You have to eat small
What's the point of
Big brothers?
Oh no, not now!
Here comes the other one!

Michaela Barton (9)
Dunblane Primary School, Dunblane

My Sandwich

I had a sandwich yesterday
It was a sandwich
So disgusting
No words can ever say
But I'll try
And tell you
As good as I can
Now let me tell you
What happened -
No, I can't!
It's too disgusting!

Jennifer Steen (9)
Dunblane Primary School, Dunblane

Bowling

Yesterday me and my family went bowling.
My dad took the first shot,
His score was three.
Next it was me, yeah, that's right,
It was my turn.
I looked down the lane to aim for the middle.
I couldn't wait any longer,
The tension was killing me.
I took my shot and waited and waited . . .
And, *wow!* I got a strike!
I'll tell you a little secret,
I've never beaten my dad before!

Alison Ross (9)
Dunblane Primary School, Dunblane

Mum, Can I Do This?

'Mum, can I play football?'
'No, not now.'
'Mum, can I play basketball?'
'No, not now.'
'Mum, can I play rounders with Erin in the park?'
'No, not now, Antonia!'
'Then what can I do?'
'I am on the phone!'
'But what can I do?'
'Just stop bothering me!'
'OK, Mum. But what can I do?'

Antonia Mackenzie (9)
Dunblane Primary School, Dunblane

Teachers!

Teachers shout
And teachers roar
They fall asleep
And sit and snore
The only reason
I go to school
Is so I can
See my friends
But still, school's quite cool!

Sophie Grant (9)
Dunblane Primary School, Dunblane

Dogs!

Some dogs are big,
Some dogs are small,
Some dogs are skinny,
And some dogs are tall!
Dogs like to run in the park,
And they really like to bark!

Kerry Taylor (8)
Dunblane Primary School, Dunblane

My Dream

My dream is to be high in the sky
Or run really fast
Or fly a plane
Or drive a car
Or run in a race
But most of all I like chilling out!

Daniel Willis (9)
Dunblane Primary School, Dunblane

The Dragon Poem

There was a person called Joey
Who had a pet dragon called Sophie
And she had a small body like Joey
And she had lots of spikes and a few horns
But she couldn't breathe fire
But Joey loved Sophie.

Fraser Gordon (9)
Dunblane Primary School, Dunblane

My Favourite Things

My favourite singer is Avril Lavigne,
Her songs are brill.

Roses are my favourite flower
You can get yellow, red, pink and white,
They are all bright.

Lilac is my favourite colour,
It is bright,
In the dark it makes me jump with fright.

Collies are my favourite dogs,
Their fur is soft,
They feel like the teddy in my loft.

My favourite book is Matilda,
It's exciting.
The Trunchbull is really scary,
She makes me very wary.

A cheetah is my favourite animal,
The colours are bright and it's
Fast . . .

My favourite day of the week is Saturday,
You can have long lie-ins and there is no school.

Amy McGlashan (8)
Greenloaning Primary School, Dunblane

My Favourite Things

My favourite thing
Is my Game Boy.
It makes me happy.
My favourite TV programme
Is Scooby Doo
It's funny.
My favourite CD
Is Hell's Bells.
It's noisy and cool.
My favourite sweet
Is chewing gum.
I like the taste.
My favourite sport
Is rugby.
It's fun.
My favourite animal
Is a monkey.
I like climbing trees.

Oscar Schad (7)
Greenloaning Primary School, Dunblane

My Favourite Things

My favourite possession is my black, cuddly dog.
Cuddly and soft.
My favourite dog is a Labrador.
I like them when they are puppies.

My favourite car is a Jeep.
It makes a lot of noise when the engine is on.

My favourite books are the Harry Potter ones.
Exciting.
Magical.

My favourite colour is blue.
The colour of the sky on a sunny day.

Heather Wighton (7)
Greenloaning Primary School, Dunblane

My Favourite Things

My favourite food is macaroni.
It smells lovely and it oozes cheese.
It's tasty.
Yum!

Football is my favourite sport.
It's sporty.
Fun and
Jumpy.

A tarantula is my favourite bug.
It's creepy and crawly,
Scary but cool.

My favourite colour is orange.
It's calm and nice.

PlayStation is my favourite toy.
It's great fun and looks great too.

Dip-dab is my favourite sweet.
It's sour,
Tangy
And smells sweet.

My family is my favourite possession.
They're loving, caring and I love them too.

Andrew Aschaber (8)
Greenloaning Primary School, Dunblane

My Favourite Things

Green like the green grass sparkling in the sun.
Cuddly like my cuddly dogs lying on my bed.
Me watching Snow Dogs on a Saturday morning.
These are my favourite things!

Gail Steven (8)
Greenloaning Primary School, Dunblane

My Favourite Things

My favourite dog is a greyhound.
It's soft.

My family is fun.
We do things together.

I like roses and daisies.
They are beautiful.

I like Freaky Friday.
It is freaky.

I like the sun.
It is bright.

I like George and Anna.
They are friendly.

I love to dance.
It's my favourite sport.

Jessica Duncan (7)
Greenloaning Primary School, Dunblane

My Favourite Things

My favourite flower is a snowdrop,
It makes me feel very cold.

My favourite author is Roald Dahl,
His stories are exciting.

George's Marvellous Medicine
Is totally fantastic.

Robyn is my best friend ever,
She is so kind.

Saturday is my favourite day
Because you get to relax and a long lie-in.

Maegan Barker (7)
Greenloaning Primary School, Dunblane

My Favourite Things

My room is cosy and warm,
I wish I could stay in it all day long.

I like videos like Scooby Doo
And so do other people just like you.

My rabbit is furry,
Brown, black and white.

Slugs are slimy,
They have one arm and are green like the grass.

I love my mum and dad,
I love them all (that means Karly too).

I like football,
It is fun, it is my favourite sport.

Lloyd Rumsby (8)
Greenloaning Primary School, Dunblane

My Favourite Things

My favourite colours are red and gold
They make me feel bright and warm

Athletics club is cool and fun
It keeps me fit all day long

My dog Paddy Paws
Is playful like me

Harry Potter is a thrilling book
With Lord Voldemort
Evil as can be.

Robyn Elizabeth Horton (10)
Greenloaning Primary School, Dunblane

My Favourite Things

My favourite car is a BMW.
Cool.
Relaxing.
Leather inside.

My favourite parrot is Jockey.
He's soft like a rabbit.

My favourite video is Scooby Doo.
It's scary, exciting and fun.

My favourite book is Harry Potter.
Read it - OK!

My favourite sport is football, it's cool.
The ball's in the back of the net!

My favourite CD is McFly.
They're cool, rocky and smart.

My favourite colour is orange.
It is delightful.

Ciaran Reilly (7)
Greenloaning Primary School, Dunblane

My Favourite Things

My favourite flower is a rose,
I like the smell that attracts my nose.

My favourite instrument is a flute,
I would never want it to mute.

My favourite colour is blue,
It always makes everything feel new.

My favourite game is tig,
Because I go in the trees and get some twigs.

My favourite animal is a bunny,
Because I have one of my own and I think he is very funny.

Karly Rumsby (10)
Greenloaning Primary School, Dunblane

My Favourite Things

Black reminds me of the night
Good time to have a pillow fight.

I like cricket because it's fun
And you get to run.

I like pizza because it's tasty
(Sometimes I eat it rather hastily.)

I like lilies because they're nice
But when we water them they're as cold as ice.

My favourite video is James Bond
Bond is the name of the tadpole in the pond.

My favourite photo is of my rabbit Sparks
He used to make the dogs bark.

My favourite place is the Sma' glen
Perfect place to build a but'n'ben.

My favourite animal is a rabbit
My rabbit's favourite food is carrots.

Amy-Claire Gibson (9)
Greenloaning Primary School, Dunblane

My Favourite Things

My favourite band is . . .

G reen Day are great.
R ole models to me.
E ntertaining.
E xciting.
N oisy.

D angerous.
A ction-packed.
Y oung.

Jordan Reilly (10)
Greenloaning Primary School, Dunblane

My Favourite Things

Spiders are cool because they make webs.
Macaroni is yummy.
Rachet and Clank is hard and tricky.
Green Day is good and funky.
Rabbits are cute, bouncy and soft.

Duncan Peter (7)
Greenloaning Primary School, Dunblane

My Monster

I have a monster
Who lives under my bed
He's really friendly
His name is Fred
He may seem scary
But he's really shy
He's as gentle as a mouse
And wouldn't hurt a fly

Fred is pink
With purple spots
His tail is green
With yellow dots
He has blue eyes
And a round, green nose
With claws for his fingers
And claws for his toes

Fred likes to eat
Ice cream, jelly, sweets
Chocolate bars, marshmallows
And any other tasty treats
Some monsters are big
Some monsters are small
But my monster Fred
Is the best one of all!

Michaela Netto (11)
Invergowrie Primary School, Dundee

School

At school
The teachers are cool
Follow the rule
Follow the rule

At the gate
You can't be late
Meeting your mate
Meeting your mate

In the line
It makes me fine
Standing up straight
Standing up straight

It's 3 o'clock
Time to go home
Getting out first
Getting out first.

Chelsea Craigmile (11)
Invergowrie Primary School, Dundee

The Colour Blue

The colour blue
Makes me feel peace
And the sound of the ocean

The colour blue
Makes me feel happy
And kind to people

The colour blue
Makes me feel
My heart beat slowly and gently

The colour blue
Makes me feel
Helpful and beautiful to everyone.

Jody MacGregor (11)
Invergowrie Primary School, Dundee

Air Raid

The raging ruby-red fire
Moves closer to ransacking over helpless buildings.
I see melting Brie
Trickling down in a hot stream in a grocer's shop.
Planes screeching and screaming overhead deafening your ears.
I see people fleeing to safety,
Droplets of sweat running down their spines.
I smell sizzling, luscious meat coming from the butcher's shop.
Searchlights swirling in disarray all along the sky.
I see the planes disappear yet again
And wonder how long until they come back?

Dylan Powell (11)
Invergowrie Primary School, Dundee

Daffodil

Daffodil, oh daffodil
Standing near the mill,
Blooming and blossoming,
With all free will.

Happy when the sun's up,
Unhappy when it's not,
But you keep up a smile,
Even if it's not.

When it's dawn,
In spring you're born,
To show your face to the world,
That's how you know when to show,
At the end of the wintry snow.

But when you wither,
You know you've been hither,
At the face of the world,
Now you're only a bulb,
In the ground, waiting
Another year over.

Kevin Karan Singh (11)
Invergowrie Primary School, Dundee

The Emmock View

I was walking down the road today
The sky was blue and clear
I was coming back from school that day
And I knew my home was near

In the field behind my house
The horses stood along
They knew what time of day it was
As feeding time was known

The farmer drove up to the field
With his trailer full of hay
The horses neighed and galloped down
This lovely sight I see every day

All this beauty I see from my room
And the view is priceless too
Yet Invergowrie is 20 minutes away
And, yes - I like it there too.

Jonathan Gray (11)
Invergowrie Primary School, Dundee

About A Man

The man with the plan
Eats some flan
Got out a can
And has a great tan

The boy set a flame
The man got the blame
But luckily it started to rain

The boy's name was Kane
The man said, 'You're going up the wrong lane.'
But the boy thought he was insane

The man was on the plane
He looked out the window and he saw the boy on the crane
Then he thought, *I must be insane!*

Ben Falconer (12)
Invergowrie Primary School, Dundee

Bottlenose Dolphin

You brethren of the nether sea
Who leap and play so happily
Singing songs amid the fish
Doing whate'er you will wish
I wish I could one day meet you

Most of the world does not like me
They use big nets and I have to flee
Tursiops Truncatus is my given name
Always an endless game
'Twixt the reefs and shores

When we use those fishing nets
To catch fish just for our pets
We need to think of our dolphin friend
To keep him playing till his natural end
Forever leap the dolphin, wild and free!

Susannah Cummins (11)
Invergowrie Primary School, Dundee

Friends

My friends are the best
They never let me down
All of them can make me smile
Even after a frown

They are always happy
No matter what they do
Because they are my best of friends
I know they'll see me through

I never want to lose them
They are the best things I have
None of us are ever bored
Because we're so, so mad!

Megan Syme (11)
Invergowrie Primary School, Dundee

From Old To Young

It's the first day back after Christmas
We get a letter
We burst out talking.
A week later a new teacher comes to see us
About our move
It's our first induction day
We all seem scared and anxious.
It's summer holidays
Can't believe I'm going to Harris
I'm on the bus fighting with my brothers
I'm so happy.
It's a week later
It's so challenging
It feels like yesterday
That I was in a nappy.
Meeting new friends is like a trend
It don't want it to end.

Elaine Abbott (12)
Invergowrie Primary School, Dundee

Homework

I find homework such a chore
Some of the subjects are such a bore
It's really hard to do
Maybe I could say I had the flu
Say, if I get caught
Then I'll be in trouble a lot.

I'm almost done
Just one more sum
But it's the hardest question
Anybody have a suggestion?
I've finished my homework on time
And this is the end of the rhyme.

Jack Rodger (11)
Invergowrie Primary School, Dundee

Off To The Zoo

We're off to the zoo today
I wonder what we'll see?
An elephant, a penguin
Or perhaps a manatee,
And if we get too hungry after all that fun
Then we'll have a fizzy drink
And a sticky bun.

I hope we see more animals
Before we go away
And then go to the playground
To finish off our day.
I think it's time for us to go
The day has been great fun,
I liked seeing all the animals
And loved that sticky bun.

Jennifer Glass (11)
Invergowrie Primary School, Dundee

I Am The Only Me

I am the only I
I am unique and special in every way
I don't follow anyone
I am the only I

I am the only me
I like sports and baking
I have asthma
No one in the world is the same as me
I am the only me

I am I, I am me
I am like my family and friends
But not the same
I do things with them
I am I, I am me.

Iona Currie (12)
Invergowrie Primary School, Dundee

My Football

Football is the sport I play
It's all I want to do all day
My skills improve each time I practise
When I train I learn more tactics

On Sunday I've got games to play
Each time I hope to score that day
Top goal scorer, who will it be?
Please, Lord, make it be me

When I score I'm filled with glee
The excitement always gets to me
When the game finishes we all shake hands
Then find out where in the table we stand

Football's what I do all week
To fulfil the aim that I seek
In the end I've enjoyed it
If I've won the game or lost it.

Barrie Pullar (12)
Invergowrie Primary School, Dundee

Memories

Everyone has memories
The good and the bad,
Everyone has memories
Though some of them are sad.
Everyone has memories
The old and the new.
Everyone has memories
Even you!
Some of them are like a hug
Others best swept under the rug.
Even the ones which make you cry
Go with you till the day you die.

Harriet King (11)
Invergowrie Primary School, Dundee

That Medieval Village

While I stay home tucked up in bed
The medieval waitress would be making the bread
Or in the inn the traveller's swaying
Merry with ale and not so good singing
I wouldn't like to live in a medieval village!

While I'm drifting to sleep now, oh this is nice
The milkmaid was screaming because she saw mice
Or while the foreign merchant was selling his goods
The peasant was in a very bad mood
I wouldn't like to live in a medieval village.

While I'm snoring in my sleep now, oh this is cosy
The blacksmith is feeling a bit dozy
Or while the pedlar's peddling his wares
The miller was kneeling while saying his prayers
I wouldn't like to live in a medieval village.

Christina Boyle (11)
Invergowrie Primary School, Dundee

How To Describe A Ghost

Some people say that ghosts are spooky
They walk through doors and walls.

But others say they have green eyes
The same as us
But see-through of course.

And when you're cuddled down in bed
They appear out of nowhere
Slimy and dead!

Some say they wear a white sheet
With two droopy eyes
You can't see their feet.

Ghosts can be
In lots of different shapes and sizes
Just don't get *scared!*

Dee Ross (11)
Invergowrie Primary School, Dundee

Table Tennis Tale 2005

The crowd is buzzing, awaiting the players
First comes Jim, the crowd goes, *'Booo!'*
Next comes Tim, the crowd goes, *'Wooo!'*
The crowd shouts, 'Come on, Tim!'
The commentator says, 'Let the match begin!'

Tim starts with a spinning serve,
It goes well past poor old Jim,
The next service very fast,
But Jim manages to crash it past,
Onto the bright blue table of Selcome Park.

The commentator shouts, 'Half-time.'
Everybody goes to drink some wine.
They all come back feeling so weary,
To see the second half so dreary.

Now it's time for Jim to serve,
It's a great serve right on the end.
It certainly drives Tim round the bend,
Oh no, Jim's serve has hit the net,
But all the crowd is calling it a let.

The game has finally come to an end,
'Oh no,' I whisper to my friend.
My favourite player has won the game,
But poor old Jim has lost again.

Oliver Bowen (11)
Invergowrie Primary School, Dundee

Dancing

Dancing is the thing I do
I've danced and danced since I was two
My favourite dance is Reet Petite
I like the way I move my feet.

I dance about all over the house
I'm certainly not as quiet as a mouse
I hope I dance when I'm older
It gives me confidence and makes me bolder.

Modern dance is what I like
The moves and twirls have got to be right
Sometimes I dance until I am dizzy
Then my mum gets in a tizzy.

I like to dance to a strong beat
But then I'm tired and need a seat
Dancing is good exercise
It helps me work off all the pies!

Lisa Pullar (12)
Invergowrie Primary School, Dundee

My Hamster

M aple is my hamster
Y ou should meet her

H appy days
A lot of fun
M y hamster is the best
S he is super duper
T ruly wonderful
E arly in the morning
R unning to see me.

Laura Jackson (11)
Invergowrie Primary School, Dundee

Cold, Misty Morning

The battle started on a cold, misty morning,
The soldiers were tired and yawning,
You could hear men praying as their swords were swaying,
On that cold, misty morning.

The ground was covered with a sea of red blood,
As the soldiers' feet sank into the wet, soggy mud,
All around you could smell the fear,
A young boy cried, 'Oh, why am I here?'

You could see all the different tartans of the clans,
The Redcoats putting good use to their plans,
Clouds of black smoke in the sky,
Most people would probably die.

That one young boy grasped onto his dagger,
As a Redcoat approached him with a threatening swagger,
He heard the sound of a beating drum
And wished for another day to come.

Hannah Ferrie (11)
Invergowrie Primary School, Dundee

The Talent Show

The talent show is on today.
What will all the children say
If I trip or get stage fright?
What if I . . . ? I won't . . . I might.
Maybe I might get booed,
I don't know if I should.
My classmates seem nice enough,
What if they get even more rough?
I hope I do pretty well,
Or my parents will give me hell.

Michael Ramsay (11)
Invergowrie Primary School, Dundee

The Clock

Mr Matthew built a clock
It went tick, tick, tick, tock
He put it on the mantelpiece
And hoped its ticking would never cease.

Then one sad day that shiny clock
Went tick, tick, tick, tick, tick, tick, stop!
He took it to his garden shed,
'Oh, bother! It's broken,' he said.

He figured out a screw was loose
Which fell into a cup of juice
Mr Matthew fixed the clock
Now it goes tick, tick, tick, tock!

Thomas David Walkinshaw (11)
Invergowrie Primary School, Dundee

My Cat

My old cat is 20 years
She lives a life with no fears.

She may be old but still goes out
To chase rabbits and mice about.

The dog even knows who's boss
She even scratched my mate Ross.

She is black, small and cute
And all but one white patch is black as soot.

She likes to sit on my knee
As I stroke her very gentl-y.

Dean Strachan (11)
Invergowrie Primary School, Dundee

I'm Nearly At The Moon

5, 4, 3, 2, 1, *lift off!*
Up, up, up
The clouds are fading
The sun is shading
I'm nearly at the moon.

Up, up, up
Stars are swinging
Rocks are spinning
My suit is ringing
I'm nearly at the moon.

Up, up, up
The Earth is smaller
The moon is taller
I'm nearly at the moon.

Up, up, up
The craters are greater
The landing was fainter
I'm nearly at the moon.

Ross Peter Murray (11)
Invergowrie Primary School, Dundee

Autumn

Autumn is a time
When summer and winter collide
Usually at this time you may see a rainbow
For the sun and rain talk
Time flies in autumn
To the cold and miserable weather towards the end
Cold winter looms ahead
Nothing is looking up but then again
The raincoat may prevail.

Alan Valentine (11)
Invergowrie Primary School, Dundee

Fun

Fun is yellow like the sun.
It tastes like crackle pop.
It sounds like fireworks exploding.
It smells like burning hot dogs on a summer's day.
It feels like soft feather pillows.
It looks like people having a good time.
It reminds me of swimming in the swimming pool.

Gordon Kettings (11)
Johnshaven Primary School, Montrose

Sadness

Sadness is blue like the ocean.
It smells like the salt coming from the wavy sea.
It also sounds like screaming and shouting in my head.
It takes me back to my past
And I see my sad memories over again.

Siobhan Anne Clement (10)
Johnshaven Primary School, Montrose

Fun

Fun is yellow like a sunny day.
It reminds me of birthday games in the garden.
It smells of salty beef burgers.
It feels like I'm out on the beach.
Fun sounds like a football whistle.
It tastes like vinegar on chips.
Fun looks like playing football.

Calum Tavendale (10)
Johnshaven Primary School, Montrose

Happiness

Happiness is blue like the bright sea.
It smells like a beautiful blackcurrant.
It feels like a wonderful feeling.
It reminds me of a smell of strawberries.
It sounds like a lullaby.
It looks like children laughing and playing.
It tastes like a packet of chewy sweets.

Stewart Niesh (11)
Johnshaven Primary School, Montrose

Fun

Fun is blue like the sea and sky,
It sounds like people laughing and having a good time.
It tastes like chocolate, fruit and biscuits,
It smells like fresh, green grass and brilliantly tasty food.
It reminds me of my best friends,
It looks like the still ocean at peace.
It feels like warm water running over my hands.

Alice Main (10)
Johnshaven Primary School, Montrose

Fear

Fear is black like empty nothing,
It looks like a pig's yard,
It smells like paper, white and plain,
It sounds like a pink pig snorting,
It tastes like something I've never tasted before,
It reminds me of a train, long and fast,
It feels like a long hand reaching out beside you.

Holli Smith (11)
Johnshaven Primary School, Montrose

Happiness

Happiness is blue like the dolphins swimming in the sea.
It sounds like laughter beating in my head.
It tastes like a large slice of chocolate cake.
It smells like daisies blooming in the sun.
It feels like soft, smooth ice cream.
It looks like a beautiful, bright sunset.
It reminds me of children playing, bursting full of happiness.

Connor Graham (10)
Johnshaven Primary School, Montrose

Sadness

Sadness is blue like Rangers.
It sounds like Celtic supporters in my head going,
'Oh no!' after Rangers have scored.
It smells like slimy, dead snails and slugs.
It feels like a squishy, red jellyfish.
It tastes like liquorice.
It looks like human flesh.
It reminds me of my grandma's dog who died.

Fiona Adams (11)
Johnshaven Primary School, Montrose

Happiness

Happiness is yellow like the bright sun.
It tastes like a juicy melon.
It sounds like a buzzing bee.
It smells like sweet honey.
It feels like an ice cream cone in the summer.
It looks like a hot desert.
It reminds me of a hot summer's day.

Ross Sangster (10)
Johnshaven Primary School, Montrose

Happiness

Happiness is multicoloured like the funfair or circus.
It smells like fragrant roses on a midsummer morning.
It reminds me of having fun with my family.
Happiness looks like a sunny day at the beach.
It tastes like a big bag of crisps.
It feels warm like a hug or a warm drink.
It sounds like the bell on the ice cream van
And polyphonic ring tones.

Corey Taylor (11)
Johnshaven Primary School, Montrose

Happiness

Happiness is blue like calm sea.
It reminds me of swimming in the swimming pool.
It smells like sweet, red roses in my back garden.
It tastes like drinking cold, wet water out of a tap.
It sounds like the waves crashing against the wall in the harbour.
It looks like people having fun on the beach.
It feels like diving in the harbour and swimming underwater.

Kyle Alan Mackie (11)
Johnshaven Primary School, Montrose

Fear

Fear is black like the bottom of a deep well.
It sounds like dripping blood on the shower curtain.
It tastes like strong whisky.
It smells like burning flesh,
It feels like a cold breath on your neck.
It reminds me of death.

Lynda McConnach (11)
Johnshaven Primary School, Montrose

Fun

Fun is yellow like the sun in the sky
It smells like a hot dog on a plate
It sounds like the wind blowing on the window
It looks like a football game
It tastes like chocolate on a cake
It feels like sand running through my fingers
It reminds me of golden time.

Craig Cessford (10)
Johnshaven Primary School, Montrose

Anger

Anger is red like a comet in orbit,
It sounds like people dying on the battlefield,
It tastes like rotten blood from the lying dead,
It smells like rotten food in the kitchen,
It looks like death staring you straight in the face,
It feels like a computer virus eating away the files,
Anger reminds me of the tsunami disaster,
People not being able to help their drowning children.

Billie Graham (11)
Killin Primary School, Killin

Fun

Fun is green like bright green grass.
It feels like wobbly jelly.
It looks like an opening flower.
It sounds like children laughing.
It tastes like a sweet strawberry.
It smells like a pink blossom.
It reminds me of playing in the garden.
Fun is green like bright green grass.

Sarah Lewis (10)
Killin Primary School, Killin

Silence

Silence is light blue like the empty sky,
It sounds like the emptiness of the black hole in space,
It tastes like the cool, fresh air in the morning,
It smells like sweet cinnamon on a biscuit,
It looks like a big open field in the middle of nowhere,
It feels like an angel floating above you,
It reminds me of a winter's day in a snow-filled garden,
Silence is lovely.

Jinny Dowling (10)
Killin Primary School, Killin

Happiness

Happiness is red like a big, red strawberry.
It feels like a bowl of strawberries.
It reminds me of little dogs playing.
It looks like Rangers scoring a goal.
It sounds like all the fans were cheering.

Jack Gibson (10)
Killin Primary School, Killin

Happiness

Happiness is like the fiery sun,
Like a big, red rose in a garden of Eden.
Happiness looks like a lovely fruit bowl.
It sounds like the breeze in the tropical trees.
It tastes like dark chocolate melting in your mouth.
It reminds me of a holiday in the hot, hot sun.
It is a giant, red rose in a garden of freedom.

David Macaskill (10)
Killin Primary School, Killin

Wartime

I see fallen buildings smashing to the ground,
I see fires burning the city to the earth,
I see bombs smashing down to the city,
I see guns shooting down all the people.

I hear people crying,
I hear people screaming with fear,
I hear dogs barking loudly,
I hear doomed people crying for help.

I feel frightened for the city,
I feel my finger against the trigger and yet I don't stop.
I feel pain in my leg where I was shot,
I feel blood running down my leg.

I smell gas in the air
I smell fire around the buildings,
I smell fear all round me,
I smell smoke in the air.

Conor Nisbet (12)
Killin Primary School, Killin

Soldier's Sight

Overhead planes flying fiercely by,
Big bombers roar overhead
Dreadful dead bodies lying everywhere
Soldiers sick because of the blood and bodies

Planes plunging into the ground,
Mammoth tanks tear round the streets,
Shells shatter in the sky,
Machine guns mow men down

Bullets scatter the ground
Rubble everywhere
Fire engines whiz around,
Men are feeling sad.

Oliver Dowling (11)
Killin Primary School, Killin

Wartime

Frightened soldiers, screaming, running from a ticking grenade,
The walls of muddy trenches, soldiers sliding down them.
Yelling soldiers, in agony as the bullets pierce their skin,
The commanding officer, giving the order to advance.

The whirring of machine guns as they tear apart soldiers' ranks,
Rumbling tanks, behind them everything ruined.
Hidden planes, waiting for the signal to drop their bombs,
The pounding of feet, soldiers running from the enemy.

Terror, terrified soldiers all around me,
Helpless soldiers squashing in trenches with me.
I feel the rain dripping down my back,
The muddy trench walls pushing around me.

I wish I could go home again,
Beat the Germans, *hip, hip, hurrah.*
I miss my friends and family,
Especially my wife and children.

Megan Rhys (10)
Killin Primary School, Killin

Wartime

Soldiers fighting for their lives, running from enemies,
Loud, exploding bombs,
Swift planes flying through the sky,
Tiger tanks rumbling past the houses.

Planes flying over the sky bombing the town,
Machine guns going *rat-a-tat-tat,*
Soldiers shouting as they march into war,
Air raid sirens screeching their warning.

Sadness as people get shot,
The squelching of boots in the mud,
The pain and suffering in me,
The waste of war.

Kevin McKenzie (10)
Killin Primary School, Killin

Fear

Fear is like white knuckles clenching tightly
It sounds like ghosts whooshing by
It tastes like seeds of peppers
It smells like spilling blood
It looks like a pitch-black room
With hidden obstacles you can't see
It feels like a million spikes about to crush you
It reminds me of hiding and waiting to be caught in hide-and-seek.

Dale Pritchard (10)
Killin Primary School, Killin

Anger

Anger looks red like fire,
It sounds like an exploding microwave,
It tastes like a sour pear,
It smells like smoke,
It looks like danger,
It feels like warning worlds,
It reminds me of a fiery ball.

Jordan Farquharson (10)
Killin Primary School, Killin

Laughter

Laughter is pink like your cheeks.
It smells like fresh air on a nice summer's day.
It reminds me of my friends.
It feels like the wind is blowing joy to everyone.
It looks like two red cherries in the nice summer sun.
It sounds like birds cheeping in the nice summer sun.
It tastes like an apple just picked.
So that's what laughter is, something nice for everyone.

Jessie Menzies (11)
Killin Primary School, Killin

Mice

I fell out of bed last night,
And landed in a pile of mice,
They all ran away,
Before I could say,
'Please stay and play, I want some pet mice.'

The next night it happened again,
I got one into a pen,
It got a huge fright,
And started to bite,
So I didn't keep it and call it Ben.

The next night I was very sad,
And I felt very, very bad,
I went to sleep,
Dreaming of sheep,
Because I've got a pet mouse now
And it's driving me *mad!*

Hazel Wyllie (11)
Killin Primary School, Killin

The Dog And The Frog

There once was a very big dog,
Who liked to play with a frog,
They played together,
In all kinds of weather,
And liked to sit on a log.

The dog was big and kind,
And the frog was covered in slime,
But they didn't care,
'Cos they made a great pair,
They played together all the time.

Lianne Kennedy (11)
Killin Primary School, Killin

World War II

I can see
Bright flashes when bombs blow up,
Planes zoom from down to up,
Soldiers trudge through the mud
While walking up to their enemies,
As our goldfish shake in their fake anemones.

I hear

People screaming, babies crying,
The screeching of air raid sirens, like dogs whining,
Loud bangs of explosives,
I wish I could escape this.

I feel

Worried, scared that my father will never come home,
The cold emptiness as soldiers roam,
The dead bodies lying there,
As we are safe in here.

Millie Tigwell (10)
Killin Primary School, Killin

Darkness

Darkness is black like a witch's black cat
Darkness sounds like a ghost waiting in a haunted castle
Darkness tastes like a disgusting potion made by an evil witch
Darkness smells like poisonous gases
Making me cough and choke
Darkness looks like a roaring storm raging all day
Darkness feels like being all alone in a dark room
Darkness reminds me of a dark, spooky castle
With wailing, black cats
Darkness is black like a witch's cat.

Callum Watt (9)
Killin Primary School, Killin

The Pear

There was an old pear
It had no hair
It always sat on a chair
By the time it was ripe
It fell down a pipe
And now it is no longer there.

Luke Melia (11)
Killin Primary School, Killin

The Icy Star

I'm a spiky ball.
I'm a glittering snowdrop.
I'm a shiny keyhole,
I'm a bit of silver ice.
I'm a sparkly lantern.
I'm a shiny diamond.
I'm a magic lamp.
I'm a snowflake.
I'm a star made of ice.

Hamish Duff (8)
Lethnot Primary School, Brechin

The Eagle

It flies fantastically in the air spying on its prey.
It flies in the sky like a glider hovering.
The golden eagle wanting rabbits desperately for its young.
The golden eagle's big and gold eye appears out of the wood.
It spies on a rat and puts out its talon.

Liam Howe (10)
Lethnot Primary School, Brechin

Autumn

Fluttering leaves fall from the trees,
Fighting as they fall to the soggy, wet ground.

Beech nuts falling, sycamore seeds come down slowly
Like aeroplanes in the sky.

Hard, monstrous conkers falling to the ground
In their spiky balls.

You can hear the rustling leaves
As the wind blows.

The colours of the leaves
Orange, brown, yellow, spotted, dead, dark red and all greens.

Skeleton leaves
Lie on the ground.

Heather Duff (10)
Lethnot Primary School, Brechin

Autumn

I went to shut the window,
A leaf came floating in,
It was orange and brown and crusty,
Like a rusty old pin.

The wind was howling around,
The grass was covered in leaves,
Some of them freshly fallen,
From their motherly trees.

The birds were searching feverishly,
For a scrap or crumb,
To last them through the winter,
Which was surely about to come!

Ross McLean (11)
Lethnot Primary School, Brechin

Lavy The Zarborg

Lavy is a Zarborg,
He has snakes for hair.
He is a bit slimy,
But he doesn't care!

Lavy has daggers for arms,
So he can chop off heads.
So all of you little people,
Stay in your beds!

His teeth are sharper than knives,
He's eaten all his wives.
His body's made of lava,
Oh, what a palaver!

His eyebrows are raised,
He lives in a maze.
And nobody, nobody knows!

Callum Fletcher (9)
Lethnot Primary School, Brechin

The Big Hot Air Balloon

Calmly floating in the sky,
A giant balloon flying high,
Flashy fun to see in the park.

Round, magical floating in the sky,
A blaze of fire, up it goes,
High fly, up in the sky.

It makes a shadow down below,
A flame waves into the balloon,
Floating in the race.

Megan Tait (10)
Lethnot Primary School, Brechin

A Heron

A big, tall bird standing royally beside the water.
Waiting for its tea.
Standing tall and curved is a cloudy-grey heron.
Can't find its tea, flies away and catches a bee.
Drops down and lands on the ground.
Standing still is this enormous heron waiting for its tea.
A fish flows by.
The heron is sharp and grabs it,
Flies away and gives it to its young.

Connor Gourlay (10)
Lethnot Primary School, Brechin

Ocean Of Storms

Thunder roaring in my ear,
Bright as the sun when the lightning strikes,
Storm clouds hovering over my head,
Water splashing into my boat,
I hear the echo of shouting in the breeze,
I got scared when the rain came crashing down,
The rocking boat made me feel unwell.

Ruairidh Martin (9)
Lethnot Primary School, Brechin

The Sun

The sun is a big, hot fireball,
Glowing red, orange and yellow.
It reminds me of the summer days
And playing on the sand.
If the sun was an animal,
I think it would be a roaring lion
With its orangey-red mane.

Rebecca Martin (8)
Lethnot Primary School, Brechin

Winter

Anxious faces looking through the frosted windows,
Waiting and praying for snow,
First drop falls and their faces light up.

Angels printed in the snow,
Frozen tears hanging from ledges,
White men standing frozen to the ground.

The school bells aren't ringing,
Bombs of snow are hitting,
Trails left by the racing sledges.

Children's faces glowing like candles,
Footprints pressed into the snow,
Ice is glistening like a mirror.

Winter is obviously here!

Helen Matheson (11)
Marybank Primary School, Muir of Ord

Summer Day

S ummer is fun
U nder the sun
M any children come out to play from
M onday to Sunday
E very day
R eady to go to school on the last day of summer - oh no!

D aylight disappears into the night sky
A waking to hear the morning birds
Y esterday was fun but this summer's day comes to an end.

Ryan Macmillan (11)
Marybank Primary School, Muir of Ord

Boxing Day 2004

The world awoke all drunk and hard,
Their minds were blocked and barred.
Until the news hit their ears,
That was the least of their fears.
So far away or close to home,
The waves came in a flurry of foam.
Torn down houses, swept people away,
That was 2004's Boxing Day.

Blabheinn Mackintosh (11)
Marybank Primary School, Muir of Ord

Summer

Summer is hot, everyone is in shorts and T-shirts
Paddling pools are out
Children are happy
Mums and dads are sunbathing trying to get a tan
They'd better make the most of it
It won't stay around for long.

Harley MacKenzie (10)
Marybank Primary School, Muir of Ord

Winter

Winter is very cold
Inside is nice and warm
Night-time nobody is about
The snow is falling softly
Everyone is throwing snowballs
Run around and try not to be hit.

James Macleod (10)
Marybank Primary School, Muir of Ord

Birds

Birds are flying all the time
In and out of trees
Round and round the world
Deep into the sea
Swooping swiftly.

Matthew Walling (10)
Marybank Primary School, Muir of Ord

Sun Heats

Sun heats
Under the shade
No one disturbs me.

Andrew Bisset (10)
Marybank Primary School, Muir of Ord

Time Travelling

Wouldn't it be great to travel, time travel right in the past,
I read about this in many books
But you have to go extremely fast.

Iain Stewart (10)
Marybank Primary School, Muir of Ord

Fear

Fear is black like a shadow in the night.
It feels like a hairy spider.
It smells like smoke in a house fire.
It sounds like a door slamming shut.
It looks like a witch on her broomstick.
It tastes like sour limes.

Lauren Lafferty (7)
Mount Pleasant Primary School, Thurso

Silence

It was so silent that I heard
The walls smile.
It was so peaceful that I heard
A beetle's feet on the ground.
It was so still that I sensed
The trees dancing before dawn broke.
It was so quiet that I felt
The snow falling on the roof.
It was so muted that I heard
The stars twinkle at me.
It was so silent that I felt
There was nobody there!

Ellie Mackrell (10)
Mount Pleasant Primary School, Thurso

Silence

It was so silent that I heard
The curtains brush against the radiator.
It was so peaceful that I heard
The teddies mumble to each other.
It was so quiet that I felt
The breeze outside brush against the window.
It was so still that I sensed
The moon smile to the stars.
It was so hushed that I heard
The street lights come on.

Tammy Rendall (10)
Mount Pleasant Primary School, Thurso

Silence

It was so silent that it heard
The clouds moving around the Earth.
It was so peaceful that I heard
Myself growing.
It was so quiet that I felt
My heart beating.
It was so still that I sensed
A baby snuffling.
It was so hushed that I heard
The man on the moon.
It was so muted that I heard
My sister dreaming.
I was so soundless that I thought
I was the last person on Earth.

Caitlin Souter (10)
Mount Pleasant Primary School, Thurso

Silence

It was so silent that I heard
The rain tapping on my window.
It was so peaceful that I heard
The water lapping on the rocks.
It was so quiet that I felt
The breeze through my window.
It was so still that I sensed
A baby had been born.
It was so hushed that I heard
My hair growing.

David Ross (10)
Mount Pleasant Primary School, Thurso

Hallowe'en

H airy hags whizzing on their broomsticks.
A ll the goblins are playing naughty tricks.
L arge, lurking ghosts spooking in the streets.
L ate at night Frankenstein is dancing to some beats.
O ld hooting owls flying in the moonlight.
W erewolves leaping out and giving you a fright.
E normous eyes following you everywhere.
E verywhere is dangerous - go out if you dare.
N ever go out on Hallowe'en if you want to keep your head on.

Kerri Mackay (9)
Mount Pleasant Primary School, Thurso

Hallowe'en

H airy hags have ugly faces,
A ll the witches play races,
L urching skeletons punching pumpkins,
L arge worms munching and crunching,
O wls hooting in the moonlit sky,
W itches always do bad things - why?
E vil goblins howling in the night,
E normous ghosts - what a sight!
N ever go out on Hallowe'en night, only if you dare.

Dionne Sutherland (9)
Mount Pleasant Primary School, Thurso

Hate

Hate is brown like a burnt apple pie.
It sounds like lots of loud shouts.
It smells like smelly cheese.
It looks like grey hyenas running towards me.
It feels like small, red ants crawling up my back.
It tastes like catfish.

Robert Kennedy (6)
Mount Pleasant Primary School, Thurso

Hallowe'en

H orrid stories being told.
A pples everywhere - some are old.
L ively children all around.
L ong lollipops falling to the ground.
O wls hooting in the trees.
W eird witches torturing fleas.
E ven if your sister knows, warn her.
E vil eyes stare out of every corner.
N ever go out before midnight on Hallowe'en.

Emily J Taylor (9)
Mount Pleasant Primary School, Thurso

Hallowe'en

H aunted houses spooked with fear
A ngry skeletons drinking beer
L ate at night when ghouls are out
L aughing witches are about
O ver the fence is where Frankenstein prowls
W hen you hear the hooting owls
E yes are spying at scaredy-cats
E vil hags wearing black, pointed hats
N ever go near the graveyard on Hallowe'en night.

Ben Leonard (9)
Mount Pleasant Primary School, Thurso

Hate

Hate is black like a buzzing fly because they fly around me.
It looks like a spider crawling up me.
It smells like the mud of a dried-up pond.
It tastes like the blood from my cut lip.
It feels like a bat flapping past.
It sounds like a fierce dragon roaring.

Shannon Hawthorne (8)
Mount Pleasant Primary School, Thurso

Hallowe'en

H aunted houses full of ghouls,
A re skeletons supposed to obey the rules?
L arge lanterns with pumpkins and black cats,
L ittle witches fly with bats,
O ld owls with mice in their beaks,
W hen on wooden floors listen for the sound of creaks,
E vil eyes looking at you for a fright,
E very time the best time to go out is on Hallowe'en night,
N ever go out if you're scared of the dark.

Shannon Dunbar (9)
Mount Pleasant Primary School, Thurso

Hallowe'en

H aunted houses full of hags.
A ll of them have lost their bags.
L oud banshees lurking in telephone boxes.
L arge tails belonging to foxes.
O wls overlooking girls and boys.
W eird whispering Hallowe'en toys.
E verywhere you look wizards you'll see.
E vil werewolves hiding behind trees.
N ever go out if you do not like *Hallowe'en.*

Lisa-Marie Watt (9)
Mount Pleasant Primary School, Thurso

Sadness

Sadness is red like red metal.
It sounds like sad, slow music.
It feels like a grey, rainy day.
It smells like a dustbin in the garden.
It tastes like stale, dry bread.
It looks like a muddy field.

Lucas Halliday (8)
Mount Pleasant Primary School, Thurso

Hallowe'en

H aunted houses spooked with bloodsucking bats.
A ngry demon zombies and wild cats.
L ethal, deadly, laughing witches.
L eaping hags wearing silly breeches.
O wls overlooking the people.
W itches flying around the church's steeple.
E arwigs sticking to people's arms.
E erie people with sticky palms.
N ever go out on Hallowe'en - I'm warning you!

Glenn Ferguson (8)
Mount Pleasant Primary School, Thurso

Hallowe'en

H aunted houses full of ghosts.
A ll the lanterns are on posts.
L anterns made of pumpkins are smiling.
L aughing witches - they're hairstyling.
O ld owls out for their midnight fly.
W itches eating pumpkin pie.
E vil eyes looking at people shaking.
E very witch has Hallowe'en cakes baking.
N ever be noisy because you might not come back.

Sarah Alexander (9)
Mount Pleasant Primary School, Thurso

Love

Love is pink like a pink flower in the garden
It sounds like fireworks
It feels like the soft petals of a flower
It smells like raspberries popping out from the bushes
It tastes like chocolate cake
It looks like lots of smiley faces.

Gemma Cormack (7)
Mount Pleasant Primary School, Thurso

Hallowe'en

H airy, scary skeletons clattering along the streets.
A ll the children coming home with loads of sweets.
L oud zombies dancing in the scary wood.
L ate at night Dracula looks for blood.
O ld owls flying around people's houses.
W itches wearing ragged trousers.
E normous bats flying all around the world.
E vil cats with their long tails curled.
N osy, noisy, black-haired witches, *look out!*

Connor Dunnett (9)
Mount Pleasant Primary School, Thurso

Hallowe'en

H airy, scary skeletons in their haunted house,
A pples are falling on the little mouse,
L ate at night all the hairy skeletons come out of their graves,
L aughing witches are flying about brave,
O wls were howling all night,
W itches will give you a really big fright,
E yes are spying on scaredy-cats,
E ars are flapping on the bats,
N ever go near the graveyard at night.

Savannah Sutherland (9)
Mount Pleasant Primary School, Thurso

Love

Love is red like a heart on Valentine's Day
It looks like a cat that is asleep
It smells like the scent of a lovely flower
It tastes like a chocolate cake
It feels like the soft wind blowing on your face
It sounds like birds chirping on a sunny summer's day.

Kyra Duffy (7)
Mount Pleasant Primary School, Thurso

Hallowe'en

H allowe'en is a night for a fright.
A pple dunking late at night.
L ate at night skeletons booming.
L oud witches on broomsticks zooming.
O ld zombies dancing in the alleyways.
W icked vampires with nasty tastes.
E normous eyes everywhere.
E vil cats stand and stare.
N oisy children watching witches dancing.

Daniel Sutherland (9)
Mount Pleasant Primary School, Thurso

Hallowe'en

H allowe'en is a night for a fright.
A lways have a torch that is very bright.
L anterns glowing at every door.
L ook out for zombies in case they give you a gnaw.
O wls fly over every rooftop.
W ailing bats will be there to make you stop.
E vil eyes are everywhere.
E ven though nothing is there somebody will give you a scare.
N obody comes out after twelve o'clock.

Joanne Rawson (9)
Mount Pleasant Primary School, Thurso

Sadness

Sadness is red like a blood river.
It sounds like a scary scream.
It smells like a house that has been burnt to the ground.
It looks like a much-loved pet lying dead on the ground.
It feels like a knife in your finger.
It tastes like gas running through your lungs.

Craig Wares (8)
Mount Pleasant Primary School, Thurso

Hallowe'en

H orrible cobwebs in haunted houses.
A ngry monsters going round looking for mouses.
L oopy, long witches fly around you.
L anterns lit with slimy go.
O wls hooting up in the skies.
W icked frogs hunting for flies.
E normous, weird eyes popping out everywhere.
E vil is here - go out if you dare.
N ever say that there aren't nasty things out there.

Gary Farquhar (9)
Mount Pleasant Primary School, Thurso

Hallowe'en

H airy witches on their broomsticks.
A ll giving their potions a mix.
L arge ghosts whizzing about.
L aughing with goblins - nasty and sly.
O wls flying up to the moon.
W e should maybe go home soon.
E vil vampires knocking on every door.
E erie sounds when the wolf gives a roar.
N ever come out or you'll get a fright.

Kim Anderson (9)
Mount Pleasant Primary School, Thurso

Happiness

Happiness is blue like a calm sea
It sounds like children playing in the play park
It smells like the fresh air
It looks like the green grass
It feels like soft cushions
It tastes like vanilla ice cream.

Matthew Wood (8)
Mount Pleasant Primary School, Thurso

Hallowe'en

H airy and horrid werewolves make you shiver and scream.
A ngry witches sabotaging the football team.
L arge and scary goblins playing tricks on little kids.
L onely poltergeists lifting up your dustbin lids.
O wls go bump in the night
    and banshees scream to give you a fright.
W itches and other creatures make your body go white.
E normous footprints lead you to the wolves' lair.
E vil demons like a *nightmare* will give you a scare.
N ever go out on Hallowe'en if you think you can't handle it!

Jay Stevenson (9)
Mount Pleasant Primary School, Thurso

Fear

Fear is black like a lizard swishing its tail.
It looks like wasps buzzing up and down.
It smells like lava coming down a hill.
It tastes like a disgusting pizza.
It feels like a snake coming up your back.
It sounds like a monster coming to attack you.

Andrew McGregor (7)
Mount Pleasant Primary School, Thurso

Sadness

Sadness is blue like a tear.
It feels like you're swimming in a pool of tears.
It smells like horrible dog shampoo.
It sounds like rain thumping on the roof.
It looks like a puddle on the ground.
It tastes like salty water.

Jamie McCracken (7)
Mount Pleasant Primary School, Thurso

Hallowe'en

H allowe'en night, witches laugh and lie.
A round the moon on broomsticks they fly.
L urking at houses in the night.
L ook out for the lantern's light.
O ld bats flutter and hang on trees.
W atch out for monsters or your heart might freeze.
E normous moon in the black, starry sky.
E yes bulging with dust will make you cry.
N ever say I didn't warn you!

Vicki Davidson (9)
Mount Pleasant Primary School, Thurso

Hallowe'en

H aunted houses creeping and creaking.
A hh, look! I can see them sneaking.
L antern shining late at night.
L ook out for a nasty fright.
O wls hooting, trying to scare you.
W atch out! Something's going to say, *'Boo!'*
E arache is happening with zombies shouting.
E eek! Watch they don't ruin your outing.
N ever go near - just stay away as Mr Ghosty might come out
    to play.

Kayla Ross (9)
Mount Pleasant Primary School, Thurso

Happiness

Happiness is yellow like a shining sun up in the sky.
It looks like a cat playing with its ball.
It smells like sweet roses in a forest.
It tastes like my mum's chocolate cake.
It feels like a comfy bed when I'm tired.
It sounds like people singing a happy song.

Brogan McLean (7)
Mount Pleasant Primary School, Thurso

Hallowe'en

H aunted houses full of fright
A pple dunking late at night
L oud zombies wailing about
L arge lanterns might blow out
O wls flying about trying to scare you
W ill a devil come out and say, *'Boo!'*?
E vil witches whizzing about on broomsticks
E verywhere skeletons scare children for kicks
N asty bats flying around in the dark.

Lauren Mackay (9)
Mount Pleasant Primary School, Thurso

Hallowe'en

H aunted houses are fearful and dark.
A ngry monsters lurk around the park.
L arge bloodsucking vampires are about.
L urching evil zombies *shout.*
O ld owls hoot through the night.
W hat is that flash of light?
E vil skeletons lurch around.
E normous gaps appear in the ground.
N asty witches are flying about in the sky.

Sophie Urquhart (9)
Mount Pleasant Primary School, Thurso

Happiness

Happiness sis gold like a sparking star.
It looks like a little red robin in the garden.
It smells like blossom on the tree.
It tastes like juicy oranges.
It feels like lovely butterflies' wings.
It sounds like the beating of drums.

Brandon MacLeod (7)
Mount Pleasant Primary School, Thurso

Hallowe'en

H airy, howling hags cackling along the street.
A round the town skeletons they meet.
L anterns laughing loudly in the middle of the night.
L aughing Dracula might give you a fright.
O wls hooting noisily because they are hungry.
W erewolves are hungry and their stomachs are rumbly.
E vil witches jumping off their broomsticks.
E normous bats out doing their evil tricks.
N asty banshees will give you a bite.

Callum Ferguson (8)
Mount Pleasant Primary School, Thurso

Hallowe'en

H orrid, haunted houses are scary.
A ngry monsters are loud and hairy.
L ively, lousy creatures creeping.
L ots of blood and slime seeping.
O wls howling and widening their eyes.
W itches at parties waiting for their prize.
E verywhere there's mad bats.
E normous, screeching, scratchy cats.
N ever go near or you'll be in fear.

Holly-Ann Maree Cameron (9)
Mount Pleasant Primary School, Thurso

Love

Love is red like a love heart.
It sounds like the booming bells on Big Ben.
It smells like sweet roses in a vase.
It looks like stars twinkling in the sky.
It feels like a smooth pussy cat.
It tastes like fabulous fruit salad.

Connor Murphy (7)
Mount Pleasant Primary School, Thurso

Hallowe'en

H orrible tricks happen on Hallowe'en night.
A ngry witches will jump out and give you a fright.
L anterns are flickering as the night goes on.
L ooking for all the children who are gone.
O lder people don't open their doors in case Frankenstein
is there.
W herever you go take *great* care.
E veryone is scared when all the graves are dug up.
E ven Dracula is up drinking blood from a cup.
N ever go out alone or you never know what will happen!

Gemma Mackenzie (9)
Mount Pleasant Primary School, Thurso

Hallowe'en

H allowe'en is horrid and haunted
A pple dunking and children taunting
L anterns lit up late at night
L oud children watch out for a fright
O ld owls go twit-twoo
W herever you are I'm watching *you*
E vil eyes watching everyone
E verywhere people having fun
N ever stay up late at night or you will get a great big fright.

Ryan Riddell (9)
Mount Pleasant Primary School, Thurso

Anger

Anger is red like a sore knee.
It feels like hot stuff in my chest.
It smells like smoke from a firework.
It looks like red fire.
It tastes like hot, red chilli peppers.

Marti Ross (7)
Mount Pleasant Primary School, Thurso

Hate

Hate is red like a burning hot chilli.
It feels like a mountain of toys that are going to fall from high up.
It smells like burning gas from the fire.
It sounds like loud yelling from the swing park.
It looks like a red, angry face when you have to tidy
       your bedroom.
It tastes like hot, spicy chicken curry.

Hannah Smith (7)
Mount Pleasant Primary School, Thurso

Fear

Fear is black like a scuttling spider.
It sounds like the fire siren that makes me jump off my seat.
It smells like gas coming from a pipe.
It looks like a grizzly bear chasing me.
It feels like a slug moving on your hand.
It tastes like rotten, rancid bacon.

Lucy Munro (7)
Mount Pleasant Primary School, Thurso

Fear

Fear is black like a dark night
It sounds like a werewolf howling
It feels like a vampire biting you
It smells like hot hands on fire
It tastes like mud out of the ground
It looks like a peg pinching your nose.

Grant Robertson-Carswell (7)
Mount Pleasant Primary School, Thurso

Silence

It was so silent I could hear
A spider spinning a web.
It was so silent I could hear
The world turning.
It was so peaceful that I could hear
Someone blinking.
It was so peaceful that I could hear
My cat thinking.
It was so quiet that it could hear
A feather sail through the air.
It was so quiet I could hear
Myself growing.
It was so still I could hear
The seaweed growing.
It was so hushed that I could hear
A worm burrowing in the mud.

Ryan Swanson (10)
Mount Pleasant Primary School, Thurso

Silence

It was so silent that I heard
A caterpillar munching on a leaf.
It was so peaceful that I heard
Some snowflakes falling gently on the window.
It was so quiet that I felt
The branches bang together in a swinging motion.
It was so still that it sensed
The computer screen chatting to the mouse and keyboard.
It was so hushed that I heard
A star dancing in the sky.

Amy Munro (10)
Mount Pleasant Primary School, Thurso

Happiness

Happiness is green like a new, shiny car
It feels like a big splash in the pool
It smells like hot, cheesy pasta
It sounds like a fire engine driving past
It looks like a smiley face
It tastes like fizzy fruit pastilles.

Kris Malcolm (7)
Mount Pleasant Primary School, Thurso

Happiness

Happiness is red like a hot, burning fire
It sounds like cracks of wood
It feels like soft and smooth clouds
It smells like strawberry jam on toast
It tastes like hot mint sweets
It looks like the sun shining on me.

Michael Wares (7)
Mount Pleasant Primary School, Thurso

Hate

Hate is red like a big, hot fire
It sounds like an out of tune piano
It feels like hailstones falling on you
It smells like disgusting smoke
It tastes like dustbins in the morning
It looks like someone shouting at you.

Jamie Mackinnon (7)
Mount Pleasant Primary School, Thurso

Silence

It was so silent that I heard
My posters talk to each other.
It was so peaceful that I heard
My sister breathing in her sleep.
It was so quiet that I heard
A baby grow day by day.
It was so still that I sensed
The clock face drifting to sleep.
It was so hushed that I heard
A rose petal falling.
It was so muted that I heard
Snow falling to the ground below.
It was so soundless that I felt
An oak tree sighing in the forest at dawn break.
It was so meek I sensed
Everyone open their eyes to see the morning light.

Danny Gunn (11)
Mount Pleasant Primary School, Thurso

Silence

It was so silent that I thought
The world had dropped dead.
It was so peaceful that I heard
A caterpillar eat the leaves of a tree.
It was so quiet that I felt
An electric cable vibrate.
It was so still that I sensed
A bird sleeping in his nest.
It was so hushed that I heard
The grass growing under the moon.

Steven Firth (10)
Mount Pleasant Primary School, Thurso

Silence

It was so silent that I heard
A television turn off.
It was so peaceful that I heard
My thoughts go tiptoeing out of my head.
It was so quiet that I felt
Like a hedgehog all curled up in a ball.
It was so still that I sensed
The wet leaves drop from the trees onto the slowly growing grass.
It was so hushed that I heard
Nothing except for a little bird singing gently.
It was so silent that I heard
A bluebottle buzzing in the air.
It was so dozy that I could hear
The corner shop till go *bling!*

Liam Elder (10)
Mount Pleasant Primary School, Thurso

Silence

It was so silent that I heard
The moon coming closer.
It was so peaceful that I heard
The rain dripping on the window.
It was so quiet that I felt
Like I was blowing up like a balloon.
It was so still that I sensed
Some trees were crashing together.
It was so hushed that I heard
My dog barking like mad.
It was so soundless that I heard
My rabbit smile.

Lauren Mackenzie (10)
Mount Pleasant Primary School, Thurso

Silence

It was so silent that I heard
The birds singing on the window ledge.
It was so peaceful that I heard
The wind blowing the trees back and forward.
It was so quiet that I felt
A daffodil opening.
It was so hushed that I never heard
My dog bark once.
It was so still that I never heard
A snowflake fall on the ground.
It was so creepy
That my dog jumped in his sleep.

Laura McPhee (10)
Mount Pleasant Primary School, Thurso

Silence

It was so silent that I heard
The traffic lights changing colour.
It was so peaceful that I heard
A leaf falling.
It was so quiet that I felt
A butterfly brush my cheek.
It was so still that I sensed
The birds flapping their wings.
It was so hushed that I heard
The sun setting.

Shannon Swanson (9)
Mount Pleasant Primary School, Thurso

Silence

It was so silent that I heard
The whispers of the wind.
It was so peaceful that I heard
The birds singing beautifully.
It was so quiet that I felt
A warm breeze softly passing.
It was so still that I sensed
A smell of Mother Nature's goodness.
It was so hushed that I heard
The dust softly hitting the ground.
It was so hushed that I heard
Seahorses mating.

Michaela Cameron (10)
Mount Pleasant Primary School, Thurso

Silence

It was so silent that I heard
Snowflakes drift to the ground.
It was so peaceful that I heard
A worm wriggle along the ground.
It was so quiet that I felt
A cold shiver go down my spine.
It was so still that I sensed
My dog dreaming about a hamburger.
It was so hushed that I heard
A duck in the duck pond go *quack! quack!*

Kasey Maclean (11)
Mount Pleasant Primary School, Thurso

Silence

It was so silent that I heard
The flowers opening on the bushes.
It was so peaceful that I heard
The birds talking and singing to each other.
It was so quiet that I felt
The moon going down.
It was so still that I sensed
The trees greeting each other.
It was so hushed that I heard
The sun rising up.

Rachael Canavan (11)
Mount Pleasant Primary School, Thurso

Silence

It was so silent that I heard
The rain crackling on my window.
It was so peaceful that I heard
A flower opening.
It was so quiet that I felt
The beat of a bird's wing.
It was so still that I sensed
The stars twinkling.
It was so hushed that I heard
A baby crying.

Marc Hooker (10)
Mount Pleasant Primary School, Thurso

Silence

It was so muted I could hear
The pumpkins grow with might.
It was so soundless I could hear
Through the thickest walls in the world.
It was so gentle I felt
As if I could hear Australia.
The world was so dozed I heard
Sheep call half a mile away,
The slightest rustle of a caterpillar
Eating leaves, trickling in the morning air.

Eoin McCracken (10)
Mount Pleasant Primary School, Thurso

The Angler's Dinner

Darkness echoes where it dwells,
Its light shines like a thousand suns,
Like poison to the eyes,
Undetectable until attack,
It's stalking you,
Watching and waiting,
Strike!
Pounce!
And rips you apart,
The victim of bloody murder.
My sorrow lies upon you,
As blood spills out,
Your death looms,
Closer.

Conan Gavan (11)
Netherley School, Stonehaven

Ice Skating

I skated round the ice
I felt confused
Round me professionals
No sign of a bruise
Fell on so many occasions
Tired as ever
Started to practice more
Girls doing incredible spins
Dazzling, glittering and shining dresses
Bright stripes of sequins
Twinkling and shimmering away
Is what I hope to be . . .

Rebecca Smith (9)
Netherley School, Stonehaven

Kitchen Creeper

There's a weird, creepy creature,
In my spotless kitchen,
With twitching whiskers,
And piercing eyes,
That stealthily creeps.

Most people hate him,
But intelligent he is,
As he clears our crumbs,
We adore that creepy creature,
That is a creepy mouse.

Kelly Dunn (11)
Netherley School, Stonehaven

Fireworks

Bangers booming,
Cartwheels cracking,
Sparklers shimmering,
Rockets raging,
Fountains fizzing,
Shooting stars spraying,
Glowing like a hot sun,
They light up the sky.

Lynsey Angus (9)
Netherley School, Stonehaven

Life In The Tank

Glistening black eyes,
That shine like crystals,
Beautiful golden scales,
Twinkling in the light.
Gliding like a man on the moon,
Blurry sounds from above,
Peaceful and calm in a watery world.

Ashleigh Welsh (10)
Netherley School, Stonehaven

A Ball

It's rolling down the hill at 20mph,
Bouncing, moving around, going everywhere.
Heading towards the big house at the bottom of the hill.
The orb-shaped ball bouncing higher and higher.
It bangs against the window and shatters the glass.

Andrew Junnier (10)
Netherley School, Stonehaven

How Could You Live Without A TV?

How could you live without a TV?
Films, cartoons or even Casualty,
Films can be scary,
Let me hide away,
Now Casualty's just boring,
I'm yawning, yawning, yawning,
Telly is outstanding,
Supreme and first class.

Sports are exciting,
Eyes are totally glued,
Soaps are addictive,
You can get really hooked,
My fave show,
Oh, you'll never know,
All you know is,
I couldn't live without a TV!

Stefan Michael Schmid (11)
Netherley School, Stonehaven

Frantic Friendships

There was an old man from Bombay,
He went to the beach in May,
He went for a swim till the tide came in,
Then invited his friend to stay.

When he invited his friend to stay,
They made up a classical play,
He dressed up in white
And turned off the light,
And scared his poor friend away.

Sonia Moir (11)
Netherley School, Stonehaven

School, School, School

Lots of brainy faces
Screams and shouts
Tables and chairs
Children work fast

Felt-tip pens
Paper and chalk
PE and Drama
Lots of work

Line up quickly
That's the rule
Add them up
And they equal
School!

Rebecca Booth (9)
Netherley School, Stonehaven

Cows

Running about in the shed
Afraid of the wind
The rattling roof
Mooing cows,
Clicking feet
Roaring tractors
The smell of sweet silage
The little calf pouncing around
Cattle wanting to get fed
Finally out to play.

Ian McNeill (9)
Netherley School, Stonehaven

Turning The Pages

There's different types of reading
I'm sure you've experienced it by now
There's flicking through a book
Skipping the boring parts
But my favourite type of reading
Is turning the pages with rapt attention

I can live without television
But not my enchanting books
Thick books, thin books, make-believe and true
Turning the pages of any book is what I like to do
When I read one page I'm forced to read more
To open my imagination.

Bethany Byrne-McCombie (9)
Netherley School, Stonehaven

Brightness In The Playground!

Forwards and backwards on the swing I go
Boys are playing footie
Girls are skipping, hop, hop, hop
Little ones are screaming like mad
Children creeping up on others
Boooo!
Aarrgghh!
Brightness in the playground
We play together like good friends should
The playground is an amazing place
I hope everyone has a happy playground like this!

Caitlin McMurtrie (8)
Netherley School, Stonehaven

Ice Dance

Professionals will jump left and right.
Will spin on one leg and two.
The ice will glaze like the ocean.
They will do drags, spirals and 3 jumps too.
The girls' dresses with twinkle like the sun
And they'll do lifts the whole night through.
The crowd will yell like never before
When they skate round as if they flew.

Emma Smith (8)
Netherley School, Stonehaven

The Porcupine

Spiky, dangerous, deadly mask,
Plodding along so strong,
Like a miniature monster,
With razor-sharp spikes,
Alone in the big, dark forest,
He is brave, bold and always thinking,
Gnawing, gnawing into trees.

Rachel Smart (9)
Netherley School, Stonehaven

Beasts Of The Blue

Smooth and glistening in the ocean blue.
Graceful and waving,
Searching for prey.
Slicing through water like a hot knife through butter.
Slipping through the sea like a ghost.
A spirit, a hunter stalking his prey.

Brodie Willaims (8)
Netherley School, Stonehaven

Splashing Waves

The waves splash and crash
Underneath, a watery world comes to life
Coral is sharp and smooth
The sun gleams across the ocean making fish shimmer
Rainbow fish dart about
Fish play in the bright coral
The coral is bright like a rainbow
Yellow, blue, pink and green fish shimmering
The waves splash and crash.

Laura Mann (9)
Netherley School, Stonehaven

A Windy Day

The wind is blowing
Over the hill.
The poppies are bobbing,
The tulips are swaying,
Birds are dancing
In the air,
A kite is bobbing
Up and down.

But the wind
Is singing
A sad, sad song.

Catriona Galloway (9)
Plockton Primary School, Plockton

The Mare

What can I see?
A soft coat that shimmers in the soothing, summer's sun.
Strong, powerful legs moving as quickly as lightning.
The long, wavy mane and tail moving with the silent wind.
A pair of gentle blue eyes that are as blue as crystal-clear water.

What can I feel?
A burst of joy as the beautiful and enchanting creature sweeps
                                                    past me.

A soothing breeze as it gallops gracefully past me.
The clattering of the mighty hooves hitting the ground under my feet.
My heart lifting with joy as the elegant mare stops to stare at me.

What can I hear?
Her heart is pounding hard but she does not look tired.
She snorts softly as she walks calmly and smoothly towards me.
Soft thuds as her heavy hooves hit the ground gently.
The wind rustling through her mane and her tail swishing about.

Sarah Ruth Fenn (11)
Rosehall Primary School, Lairg

Anger

Anger is red like a blazing fire,
It looks like a furious bull,
It feels like a spiky surface,
It smells like a dirty pig,
It sounds like a stampede of elephants,
It tastes of a raw fish,
It reminds me of fighting over rules.

Simon Fenn (9)
Rosehall Primary School, Lairg

Snow

I see a big, white, fluffy cat,
Her name is Snow, she wears a hat,
She's big and round and likes to play,
She keeps Mum busy all though the day,
She's on the table and licking the plates,
And she's always scratching on our gates!

I hear screeching, what's she done now?
I'll go and see. *Oh no!* but how?
She's smashed Mum's china, she's ripped my book,
My mum comes in, I said, 'Don't look!'
Suddenly she saw it, looking at all the mess,
Mum's great big smile getting less and less.

I feel like screaming, 'Now I'm in trouble!'
Then Dad came in, make that double,
Dad came in and saw the mess
And *his* big smile got less and less,
While I got the row for little Snow's clutter,
Snow was in the kitchen eating the butter.

Sophie Marie Baillie (10)
Rosehall Primary School, Lairg

Love

Love is pure red hearts in the air,
It smells like a lovely red rose,
It looks like a beautiful picture,
It tastes like sparkly pure air of flowers,
It sounds like the birds are singing,
It feels like you are a beautiful rose,
It reminds me of marriage.

Hannah Ekema (8)
Rosehall Primary School, Lairg

Cool Cats

Tiger's stripes out of the corner of my eye,
I keep on praying, will I die?
She takes down a male deer with huge horns,
Her massive teeth look like spears or thorns,
She enters the bushes with the deer,
I hope she can't see me here!
Wow! There's a cub and another and another!
She must be a very, very proud mother.

The tigers are running towards me!
I hope they've all eaten their tea!
One of the cubs gets nearer and nearer,
The mum is coming, I can hear her,
The cub scampers off but Mum's tail gets caught,
I hesitated to help but then I thought,
Yes I will, 1, 2, 3,
Wow! She's heavier than a tree!

Her fur is so smooth and soft,
She is taller than my house and loft!
I could tell she was worried because her child,
Was running around in the dangerous wild,
The other two were rolling and making noise,
Like a young toddler playing with toys,
Her tail gently swiped my face,
Zooming, I ran back to base.

Hannah Louise Stevens (10)
Rosehall Primary School, Lairg

Happiness

Happiness is pink like bunny rabbits' ears,
It sounds like a great tit singing,
It looks like children with no fears,
It tastes like a bolognaise sauce,
It smells like a bunch of flowers,
It feels like a soft and warm blanket,
It reminds me of my old school friends.

Liah Beth Stevens (8)
Rosehall Primary School, Lairg

Darkness

Darkness is black like the midnight sky,
It smells like the winter air,
It tastes like the coldest ice cube,
It sounds like howling wolves,
It looks like the fur of a black bear,
It feels like a frozen shadow,
It reminds me of being in a deep sleep.

Liam Spence (9)
Rosehall Primary School, Lairg

Fun

Fun is gold like the golden sand,
It smells like a big bunch of roses,
It sounds like children's laughter,
It looks like exotic rides,
It feels like stars sprinkling over you,
It tastes sweet like happiness flowing through your body,
It reminds me of laughing with my friends.

Jordan Morrison (11)
Rosehall Primary School, Lairg

Tea Time

Slimy snails in your food,
Squiggly worms in Christmas pud.
Warty toads in your sweets,
And flies crawling on your meats.
Rats nibbling on fried rice,
If there is not enough they eat the mice.
Maggots crawling on your spoon,
Upset stomach coming quite soon.

Juman Hamza (11)
Stracathro Primary School, Brechin

Space Invasion

Outer space, it's everywhere,
You can't escape from its wide stare,
The aliens rule from planets afar,
From every comet to every star.

The planet Mars is their main base,
No human has seen one face to face,
The aliens will be with us to the end,
And they are definitely foe not friend.

The humans can try and try again,
But our technology will never beat them,
We can try and try and spend and spend,
But they're much too hi-tech in the end.

So you should watch out for UFOs,
Especially since they are our foes,
Aliens are coming to attack planet Earth,
And are looking for a place to make their berth.

Innes Cuthill (10)
Stracathro Primary School, Brechin

Our Dog Archie

Archie is our dog,
He loves all his treats,
All the bones and biscuits,
Also the left-over tea.

Archie is so playful,
He really is a charm,
He plays with all his doggie pals,
Then they run all around.

We love Archie very much,
We call him little, cute names,
He really loves us too,
Also the fun and games.

Katie Blewitt (10)
Stracathro Primary School, Brechin

That Lazy Guy!

There is a guy across our street,
And all he does is eat, eat, eat,
Chicken, turkey and kidney pie,
All the cooking makes his wife sigh.

For she is the one who washes the dishes,
Although she really and truly wishes,
That she could not be related to this awful man,
So she packed her suitcase and off she ran.

So I bet you are wondering what happened to the guy,
The guy who made his ex-wife sigh,
He left his house in search of a wife,
He wanted to lead a different life.

But as he was walking across the street,
A car came and knocked him off his feet,
So now he lies down, dead, asleep,
Trying to remember how to count sheep.

So a warning to all who read this verse,
Eating too much is an evil curse,
So don't eat much chicken or any pie,
Don't eat too much or you'll be saying goodbye!

Rosie Wilkinson (10)
Stracathro Primary School, Brechin

The Old Dragon

There was an old dragon,
He took a big sigh,
He was a thousand years old,
And he flew up into the sky,
That dragon was too old,
And he flew too high,
He fell to the ground,
And he lay there to die,
He thought, *Oh well!*

Katie August (10)
Stracathro Primary School, Brechin

Weather

The snow falls gently on the ground,
Landing, making not a sound.
It lands on the grass, on the gate,
So if it's thick I go sledging with my mates.

The rain, it's an awful pest,
No point in wearing your Sunday best.
If it's heavy it can cause a flood,
And creates a landslide with lots of mud.

But there is a saviour called the sun,
Imagine lying on the beach with a burger bun.
Shining brightly in the sky,
Oh, what a heat, my, oh my!

Yes, it's typical British weather,
You couldn't get anything better.
The rain, the snow and the sun,
We've got all three not just one!

Emma Ewen (11)
Stracathro Primary School, Brechin

My Uncle Scott

My uncle Scott is very nutty
He is always cheeky to my mummy
And he likes to play with putty
And he has a very fat tummy.

My uncle went to work one day
To earn some money for his wife
But his car broke down over the Tay
So he had to get help before he lost his life!

When my uncle got back home
His wife was very upset
So he was banned from his mobile phone
Until he had paid his debts!

Ashley Spark (10)
Stracathro Primary School, Brechin

I'm Gonna Be An Astronaut

I'm gonna be an astronaut and fly to outer space,
I'll have a hi-tech rocket and a smile upon my face.
I'll bring my best friend Emma, we'll build a space hotel!
Then all our friends and family could come up there as well!

We'll do the moonwalk on the moon and nickname all the stars,
We'll fly to visit Jupiter and have our tea on Mars!
We'll make friends with the aliens and play tig on Saturn's rings,
Then they'll fly back home in the UFOs thinking happy things.

So once we're a little tired we'll fly back to our hotel.
Guess what! It has an en suite and a lounge room as well!
We'll lie back in our recliners watching Garfield on DVD.
We'll get a real good view of it on our plasma screen TV!

So I wanna be an astronaut,
The most famous ever,
Now I think if I had the chance,
I'd stay up there forever!

Then again, maybe I could be an author!

Imogen Sherrit (10)
Stracathro Primary School, Brechin

I Never Said Goodbye

I was happy and I was sad
I learned easy things and I learned hard
I learned not much to fill my brain
It was one of those days where I was sad
I held my mum's hand and walked along the linchbare Path
I cried inside myself
I did not tell anyone at all
Do you want to know why I was sad?
I had to move school and that is why I was sad.
I had left my friends behind me and never said goodbye.

Shaney Allan (12)
Stracathro Primary School, Brechin

Out In The Playground

Out in the playground,
Three times a day,
Me, the boys and the girls play.

The boys play football,
The girls skip,
A P1's crying after a trip.

The girls tell secrets,
Boys tell jokes,
But a few sometimes wickedly provoke.

Mrs Taylor, she's in charge,
She watches us all through the day,
Especially when we come out to play.

She's OK!

Cameron Leask (10)
Stracathro Primary School, Brechin

Pink Or Blue?

I used to wish I had a baby cousin,
Especially a little boy,
I wouldn't have minded a little girl,
But I'd rather it was a boy.

But then the day had come,
The day my wish came true,
I was so excited,
Should I buy pink or should I buy blue?

I started to count the months,
Until the bump appeared,
Was it pink or was it blue?
What? *Triplets?* How weird!

Linzi Box (12)
Stracathro Primary School, Brechin

Celtic FC

Celtic are cool
Celtic are great
Best team in Scotland
Oh, I wish they were my mates

Out of Europe
Don't really care
Best player? Stilian Petrov
Oh, Celtic are the best

Manager O'Neil
The best Scotland's ever seen
He always knows what he's doing
So Celtic are the team

But best player left
It's a horrible shame
He moved to Barcelona
Henrik Larsson is his name.

Sam Blewitt (12)
Stracathro Primary School, Brechin

Where I Want To Stay

Far, far away
That's where I want to stay
With no one in the way
Just me - far, far away
I would bring my dog
We'd chase a frog
We'd chase a hog
We'd dance in the sun
In the sun we'd have fun
Sharing a burger in a bun
That's where I'd want to stay.

Kylie Higgins (10)
Stracathro Primary School, Brechin

Teachers

Teachers are rotten,
Teachers aren't fun.
They buy a wicked car,
And should be overrun.

They give you hard work,
They give you hard Maths.
What will they next give me?
Next in class.

The janitor is horrible,
He never does his work.
He leaves the rubbish lying,
And he really is a jerk.

I really hate this school,
And all the people in it.
Especially the teachers,
And the evil janitor.

Rosie Letham (11)
Stracathro Primary School, Brechin